Battlegro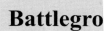

The Somme
1916

Battleground series:

Battleground

The Somme 1916

Touring the French Sector

David O'Mara

Series Editor
Nigel Cave

Pen & Sword
MILITARY

First published in Great Britain in 2018 by
Pen & Sword Military
an imprint of
Pen & Sword Books Ltd,
47 Church Street
Barnsley,
South Yorkshire, S70 2AS

ISBN 978 147389 770 0

A CIP catalogue record for this book is
available from the British Library.

Typeset in Times New Roman by Chic Graphics

Printed and bound in England by
CPI Group (UK) Ltd., Croydon, CR0 4YY

Pen & Sword Books Ltd incorporates the imprints of
Pen & Sword Archaeology, Atlas, Aviation, Battleground, Discovery,
Family History, History, Maritime, Military, Naval, Politics,
Railways, Select, Social History, Transport, True Crime,
Claymore Press, Frontline Books, Leo Cooper, Praetorian Press,
Remember When, Seaforth Publishing and Wharncliffe.

For a complete list of Pen & Sword titles please contact
PEN & SWORD BOOKS LIMITED
47 Church Street, Barnsley, South Yorkshire, S70 2AS, England
E-mail: enquiries@pen-and-sword.co.uk
Website: www.pen-and-sword.co.uk

Contents

Introduction

'Oh, No! Not <u>another</u> book on the Somme!'

With the absolute glut of narratives that have been published on this battle in the English language since the actual battle itself but, especially, over the past twenty years, and combined with the amount of TV, radio and media coverage (of varying degrees of accuracy), I must admit that would probably have been my first reaction too. However… this book intends to be different.

The vast majority of publications would have us believe that the Battle of the Somme was a British battle, not the British-French battle that it was at first intended (and, indeed, actually did become). Many narratives of the battle only ever give a passing reference to the French – some not even acknowledging that a battle even took place to the south of the river or just giving up a paragraph or two to the entire French effort. Even the French Official History only dedicates about three and a half pages to the actual events of 1st July (though, to be fair, the coverage of the rest of the battle and the lead up to the attacks is much more thorough). This book is the opposite and intends to redress the balance in what was, in all reality, a battle that was fought by the British and French in roughly equal measures. Being about the French sector, it is intended for it to be just about that – the French. There is little reference to the British on the Somme in these pages as there is plenty of other reading material about them 'out there'. However, 'out there', there is precious little reading material about the other half of the Somme battle, especially in the English language. Hopefully, this book (and its subsequent volumes, covering the French occupation of the Somme battlefields from 1914 through to 1916) will serve to redress that balance a little and, though this volume is for all intents and purposes a battlefield guide book intended to serve as an introduction to the French battlefield rather than a history, it will enable the reader to obtain a more complete picture of those events of a hundred plus years ago.

The tours section will also enable the reader to visit a much ignored section of the battlefield armed with enough information to be able to spend at least a couple of days in this sector whilst, perhaps, visiting the more well trodden paths of the British sector. Covering some of the most picturesque areas of the whole battlefield, with other areas affording wide and stunning views (and, all the while, the visitor being less bothered by crowds), many of the roads, tracks, copses and woodlands are located in the same places as they were in 1916, even if one village has 'moved' slightly and another, a hamlet, has disappeared off the face of the earth entirely. It is an extremely 'readable' battlefield and a very worthwhile detour.

Introduction by Series Editor

For some years it has been a hope of mine to find an author who could take on the task of writing books in this series on the French army during the Great War. In the recent past, largely thanks to Jack Sheldon, it has been extended to the German army and in many cases we have been able to provide at least some views from the 'other side of the wire'. However, the army that had taken on the major burden of facing the Germans for most of the war has generally, with one or two honourable exceptions, had to make do, at best, with a few paragraphs here and there in most Anglophone accounts, and certainly not least as regards the Somme. The Somme battlefield has, quite understandably, been dominated for British readers by the story of the BEF. What has made the situation even more unfortunate is that there is little, almost shamefully little, in French – the exception is the new Michelin guide to the Somme battlefield, *The Battlefields of the Somme*, the English language version of which came out in 2016.

Therefore I was delighted to come across Dave O'Mara on the Great War Forum, where his posts showed a deep knowledge of the French army during the war. With a certain amount of arm-twisting, he has assumed the task of describing the role of the French on the Somme before and during the battle of 1916. This book will be the first of five by him which will provide an English speaker with an overview and then a detailed examination, accompanied by numerous tours, of the performance of that army on ground which is well known to so many British visitors.

This gap in coverage has always struck me as leaving a void, both for the battlefield visitor and for the general reader, in our understanding of the complexity of this, the most bloody battle of the Great War. William Philpott, in his very important book *Bloody Victory* (2009), provided a balanced coverage of the Somme, giving the French contribution due weight. However, in general, you would be hard pushed to know, not least on the ground, that the French suffered 200,000 casualties in the battle, of whom some 80,000 were killed; France eventually provided almost as many troops as the British and perhaps came closest to breaking the German defences in the dying days of the battle in the utterly ferocious fighting around Sailly-Saillisel and Bois St Pierre Vaast, north of Péronne.

This first book on the French on the Somme covers the whole period from the arrival of the war in the area through to the end of the battle, from Serre in the north to Chaulnes in the south. The years of war before the British arrived included extensive underground fighting, especially on Redan Ridge, in the Glory Hole at La Boisselle, on the high ground above Fricourt, along the line between Fay, past Dompierre and towards Frise. There were instances of intensive fighting once the line had settled down, by early October 1914, for example at Serre-Hébuterne in June 1915, at Ovillers-La Boisselle (and Mametz) in the winter of 1914 and at Frise in January and February 1916.

And then there was the battle itself; although the French effort at the start of the fighting was concentrated to the immediate north of the Somme and for a few kilometres south of the river, the emphasis soon became centred on the north bank. It should be quite evident to anyone with the smallest appreciation of the practicability of military operations that progress south of the river, short of a complete German collapse, were going to be halted by the course of the River Somme, which takes a sharp, almost ninety degree, turn to the south close to Péronne. It should come as no surprise, therefore, that the French were able to do so well on 1 July 1916 in this south bank area – not only had the Germans moved a sizeable number of troops north but they could read a map.

It is my earnest hope that this book, and the ones to come on the same subject, will encourage future British visitors to extend their tours south of the river and visit this important, neglected ground, which offers so much in terms of understanding the progress of the battle and of seeing the evidence of it on the ground (at locations such as Soyécourt) and of the cost of it all, as shown by memorials and the several French National cemeteries (for example at Lihons and Dompierre), as well as that of the Germans (at Vermandovillers). By doing this they will not only be honouring the memory of the French who fought here but will also add an important perspective to their understanding of the operations of both the BEF and the Germans during the Somme 1916.

The *poilu* on the Somme has now got another spokesman; Dave's book will, I hope, bring his, the *poliu's*, contribution, his suffering and his sacrifice to the attention of many more people.

Nigel Cave
Beaumont Hamel, October 2017

Acknowledgements

This book, and its subsequent volumes, is the product of over thirty years of battlefield visits and personal study – the past fifteen or so of which have been uniquely focussed on the battlefields of the French Army. Throughout that period, I had hoped that someone would have written a book such as this (it would have made life so much easier!), but it was not to be. For just that reason, the first of my acknowledgements should go to the series editor, Nigel Cave… first for press-ganging me into writing it in the first place. Originally, I was simply in contact with him to offer up the archive of information and files that I have amassed over the years in order to assist whoever it was going to be who would be writing this book. It was only after a few email exchanges that I sussed on to the fact that it would actually be me who was going to write it. Secondly, I am grateful for all the encouragement and support he has given me throughout the process, plus the breathing space when I needed it the most!

I would also like to thank my good friend and 'man on the ground', Dave Platt, of Beaumont Hamel View guest house, Auchonvillers (http://www.beaumonthamelview.com). Not only did Dave assist me by giving me a temporary reprieve from our joint projects to enable me to concentrate on this book, but he took many of the modern day photographs that you will see in the pages to come and also drove some of the tours for me, assessing their suitability for a variety of vehicles. Dave's guest house comes highly recommended (see some of the rave reviews on his website), as do his bespoke battlefield tours – which, tailored to the choice of the individual client, can be focussed upon specific actions, units or people.

Further thanks must go to my wife, Anita, for all the encouragement in the writing of this book and for her patience and understanding whilst dragging her to yet another battlefield on a regular basis. (Slightly lesser thanks go to my two boys, Billy and Harrison, and my dog, Eric, who, I think, all enjoyed being there and accompanying me on endless evening rambles in the middle of nowhere anyway).

Honourary mention should go to Mick Blackburn (whose constant nagging for a first edition of this book encouraged me to write faster… just to shut him up!) and also to the members of the Western Front Association, East Lancashire Branch, for all the support, especially: Andy

Gill, Andy Mackay, Alan Mackay, Dave Drury, Brian Hirst and Pete Wilshaw, for all the years of encouragement in various projects, not just this one.

Finally, and by no means lastly, I have to thank, perhaps the most influential people of all involved in the writing of this book, my parents, Brian and Joyce O'Mara. After buying me a copy of *Before Endevours Fade* as a childhood birthday present and taking me on my first fourteen or fifteen trips over to the Western Front (around Ypres, the Somme, Arras, Mons, the Argonne, St. Mihiel and Verdun amongst others if my memory recalls correctly) into the 1980s they did everything they could to encourage and nurture my growing interest over the years to come. Thanks, you two. If it was not for you, this book would never have been written (well, not by me anyway!).

List of Maps

Chapter One

Soldats citoyens:
An introduction to the French Army
up to the Battle of the Somme

French artilleryman of a régiment d'artillerie lourde à grande puissance 'christening' his Canon de 240 L Mle 1884 prior to the commencement of the preliminary bombardment, June 1916.

Heavily reorganised in the years following defeat in the Franco-German War of 1870-71, the French Army immediately began reforms within a year of the conclusion of that war. Driven less by the need for revenge than it was by a desire for national defence, between 1872 and 1905 a series of laws were adopted that created a mandatory, universal, full time military service for all citizens of the Republic. An initial five years of full time service was reduced to three years in 1889 and was a situation that remained until 1905, when it was lowered to just two years. Due to fears regarding the potential size of the army should mobilisation be necessary, this compulsory military service was reinstated to three years in August 1913 (by the early mobilisation of the *classe* of 1913 rather than the extension in service of the *classe* of 1910, who were approaching the end of their full time service at that time).

The mobilisation *classe* of each soldier usually (though not always) corresponded to the year in which he celebrated his twentieth birthday. In other words, the *classe* of 1909 would, in the main, have been born in 1889, the *classe* of 1914, in 1894, etc. Following registration at his local *mairie,* the recruit was usually called into full time service locally during the autumn intake following his twentieth birthday. There were a number of reasons why service could be deferred to a later time, including a failure to make the grade medically (this would be followed by a periodic re-assessment in the years following), being engaged in higher education, being employed in a job in which military service could prove detrimental, or an older sibling being still in service. Medical failure in which it would seem that an improvement would be unlikely could lead to a lesser service in the *service auxiliaire*, which provided ancilliary services to the military. Annually, approximately 250,000 young men, representing about 33% of any given *classe* year, were conscripted into full time military service during their correct intake. A further 18% entered service at other times due to voluntary enlistment or deferred service.

Full time service was followed (from 1913) by ten years as an active army reservist, seven as a *territoriale* and, finally, another seven on the *Réserve de l'armée territoriale*, before a soldier was released from all commitments at the age of 47 or 48 (total commitment between 1889 and 1913 totalled twenty five years). Because of this system a very rapid mobilisation of an *Armée active* of approximately 1.7 million trained soldiers from all walks of life could be enabled at any given time.

Due to the nature of French conscription, whereby each regiment was allocated a home garrison and recruited almost exclusively from the districts around the vicinity of this garrison, whole groups of young men from any given area would have enlisted in the same regiments consecutively. Groups of classmates, workers in the same factories and farm hands from the same fields would have served together during their compulsory service, giving many of the French regiments a feel similar to the British 'Pals' battalions raised at the start of the Great War. Many of these men, along with their older (or younger) siblings, friends and colleagues were recalled into service together at the start of the war. Many hundreds of these men also died together in the first bloodlettings of the war, such as on the bloodiest day in French Army history: 22nd August 1914, when, during the Battles of the Frontiers, 27,000 Frenchmen mainly of the *classes* of 1911, 1912 and 1913, were to die in action, devastating whole communities. By the time of the battles of Verdun and the Somme, however, this regional aspect of most regiments had been lost as men were drafted into regiments from all over France.

At the time of the French mobilisation on 1st August 1914, the active French Army consisted of approximately 823,000 regulars, colonials and conscripts (*classes* of 1911, 1912 and 1913). Within the first fortnight of August 1914, all of the reservists of the *classes* between 1900 and 1910 inclusive were mobilised, as were all of the *territoriales* of *classes* 1893 to 1899 inclusive. By the third week of August, the size of the French Army (active, reserve, territorial and territorial reserve) had swollen to just under 4.2 million men and, by the end of the year, the young men of classes 1914 and 1915 and the 42 year olds of the *classe* of 1892 (the youngest *classe* year of the *Réserve de l'armée territoriale*) were also in uniform and on full time service. Throughout the war, the French would eventually fully mobilise all *classes* between 1888 and 1919 and partially mobilise that of 1887. By July 1916, the French Army had decreased in size to about 2,234,000. This decrease was mainly due to casualties but, to a lesser extent, it was also due to the French policy of releasing certain soldiers back to civilian life to engage in necessary war work in factories or to work on family farms etc.

Other than the system of national service enabling the rapid fielding of a massive army, the French Army, after a period of disorganisation and scandal during the final years of the nineteenth century, had also undergone a system of modernisation, becoming the first army to adopt the smokeless cartridge in 1887 (though this rifle was still in use at the outbreak of war, it was rapidly, due to its awkward tubular magazine, becoming obsolete by then), developing what was, perhaps, the finest field artillery piece of its time – the *Canon de 75 modèle 1897* and, in 1914, was also one of the few armies to be able to enter the field with a full range of hand grenades (high explosive, incendiary and chemical). A great deal of emphasis had been placed on mechanisation, rail transportation and cartography during the years immediately prior to the war and a number of specialist training schools had been set up that were open to all ranks who showed aptitiude. Combined with its recent experiences in wars in Morocco, West Africa, China, Benin, Indo-China, Madagascar, Chad/Sudan, Tunisia and Algeria during the previous thirty years, in which the French had learned lessons and adapted tactically, this modernisation made the French Army one of the most effective in the world by 1914: a fact that did not go unnoticed in Germany. Its adaptability would come into great use during the war.

Entering the war in what could be regarded as a very antiquated uniform of (for the infantry) *garance* red trousers, 'iron blue' great-coat and, though covered by a dark blue cloth cover, a red topped képi (units such as *chasseurs* and *artillerie*, dressed completely in dark blue were less conspicuous), and using outdated tactics against machine guns and artillery in open formations, the French rapidly learned their lessons and adapted quickly to the situation. Uniforms were toned down and covered, eventually evolving into the *bleu horizon* that would survive into the late 1920s and 1930s, camouflage was pioneered (the French would become one of the leading lights of camouflage during the war) and equipment and weaponry developed to be specific for certain roles. The French were the first to adopt a modern style steel helmet, replacing the steel *cerveliere* that had been worn under the képi since 1914, in June 1915 and, as the war continued, began, independently of the British, to develop tanks, eventually producing the first 'modern' style tank with a rotating turret. They were also the first army ever to issue a true self-loading rifle as a standard issue rifle, though, due to production costs and abilities, this was never going to be able to be a universal issue whilst the war was in progress and, even though it went through two different marks, only saw limited production. (Conversely, during the 1930s, the French would also become the last major military power independently to develop and adopt a bolt action rifle as standard issue after the automatic rifle project was shelved following the conclusion of the Great War).

Battle tactics into 1915 continued to be extremely costly in terms of casualties and eventually adapted and developed into the small, independent unit fire and manouvre tactics that served the French so well in the early days of the Somme Battle and are still taught in Infantry Battle Schools to this day, along with artillery tactics that would not be copied by the British for another year. True 'shock troop' tactics that would become *de rigueur* in 1918 and beyond were also being experimented with in various guises by the French Army on the Somme in 1916.

By the time of the Battle of the Somme, the French Army was a highly experienced, battle hardened modern army. Of the units taking part on the first day, all of the regiments north of the river had seen action since 1914 and had fought at such battles as the Frontiers, Picardy, the First Battle of Ypres, Artois, the Second Battle of Champagne and Verdun. Those to the south, though none had seen service at Verdun, had all fought at the Second Battle of Champagne, many also having been involved in the First Battle of Champagne or on the Wöevre or Argonne too; one had even seen service at Gallipoli. These units were all full of veterans, with even the newest intakes of recruits to these units (the *classe* of 1916) generally having seen some sort of major action (the *classe* of 1917 had only just begun to arrive and would get their turn later in the battle). Though they would be tested to the extreme following on from the first days of the Somme to the end of the battle, the hardy French mentality and the ability to absorb casualties and bravely and stoically press on continued throughout the battle.

Organisation of the The Metropolitan Infantry 1914-16

The Infantry Regiment (*Régiment d'infanterie*)
1914

There were 173 active regiments of line infantry (numbered 1 to 173) in August 1914, each comprising three *bataillons* (apart from the *69e, 157e, 159e, 163e, 164e,165e, 166e, 170e* and the *173e Régiments d'infanterie*, which were all made up of four *bataillons*). Each *bataillon* comprised of four *compagnies* that were correspondingly numbered (the *1e bataillon* consisting of the *1e* to *4e compagnie*, the *2e bataillon* consisting of the *5e* to the *8e compagnie*, and the *3e bataillon* comprising the *9e* to the *12e compagnie*), plus one machine gun section. There were also, within the *régiment*, additional units, such as the regimental general staff, the battalion staff, the Headquarters company and regimental supply train, bringing up the full strength of a *régiment* to approximately 3,250 officers and other ranks.

All of these active regiments were supplemented with a corresponding reserve regiment, consisting of two battalions. These reserve regiments were numbered accordingly with their parent regiment by taking their parent unit's number and adding 200. For example, the reserve regiment of the *70e Régiment d'infanterie* was the *270e Régiment d'infanterie*, the reserve regiment of the *141e Régiment d'infanterie* was the *341e Régiment d'infanterie*, etc. In total, therefore, there were 346 *Régiments d'infanterie* in 1914. Within the reserve regiments, *bataillons* were numbered *5e* (*17e* to *20e compagnies*) and *6e* (*21e* to *24e compagnies*).

Totally separate from their parent units, these reserve regiments did not serve alongside them and, generally, served in reserve divisions; but two regiments were placed as reserve regiments for each active *Corps d'armée*.

The final type of *Régiment d'infanterie* in 1914 was the *Régiment d'infanterie territoriale*. In 1914, there were 145 (numbered 1 to 145) territorial regiments, made up of 35 to 41 year old men and 148 reserve territorial regiments (numbered 201 to 347, 500 and 501), made up of 42 to 47 year olds (the latter age group only being called into full time service if they possessed a particular skill or who had been engaged in a specific trade). *Régiments d'infanterie territoriale* were composed of three or four battalions, one for each subdivision of the region from which they originated, but some consisted of as many as seven or as few as two.

1915

Three new regiments (the *174e, 175e* and *176e Régiments d'infanterie*) were formed at the start of 1915, two of which were destined for service at Gallipoli and Salonika, and a further twenty (numbered 401 to 421) were formed within a few weeks of these. With the exeption of the 419e *Régiment d'infanterie,* the numerical designation was attained this time by adding 400 to the army corps region number from where the regiment originated. These new regiments were composed almost entirely of new recruits (*classe de 1915* and *1916*) and bolstered by a number of veteran soldiers and non-commissioned officers transferred from other regiments (plus recovered soldiers returning to service from woundings).

Due to the massive number of casualties sustained in 1914 and 1915, alterations to the regimental structure had to be made. *Compagnie* size was reduced from 250 to 200 men and *bataillons* were reduced to three *companies* (reducing the effective strength of a bataillon from 1000 men to 750). Reserve regiments were totally separated from their parent units and became completely independent units (though the two battalion organization of reserve regiments would still remain in place for the time being). Detachments of grenadiers were also created at the company level. Consisting of sixteen men led by a non-commissioned officer, eight of these (led by a corporal) were trained as bombardiers, becoming familiar with the operation of a number af varied light trench weapons, such as catapults and light mortars, along with training in the use of hand grenades. The number of machine gun sections within the regiment was also increased to four and reorganised into an autonomous machine gun company.

1916

Manpower shortages from the spring of 1916 led to the disbanding of six of the new regiments that had been created in 1915 (*402e, 405e, 406e, 419e, 420e* and *421e Régiments d'infanterie*) and two reserve regiments from each reserve division (seventeen in total).

In April 1916, a third *bataillon* (numbered the *4e*) was added to many of the reserve regiments, which began to mirror the structure of the active regiments. *Compagnie* structure was also reorganised, with each *section* being split into two separate *demi-sections*, each made up of two rifle squads, a machine gun squad and a bombing squad. Two additional machine gun companies were created, bringing the total to three per regiment and, eventually, totally replacing the fourth rifle company. Additionally, each battalion was issued with a 37mm *Canon d'Infanterie de 37 modèle 1916 TRP* infantry support gun, which fell under the control of the machine gun section.

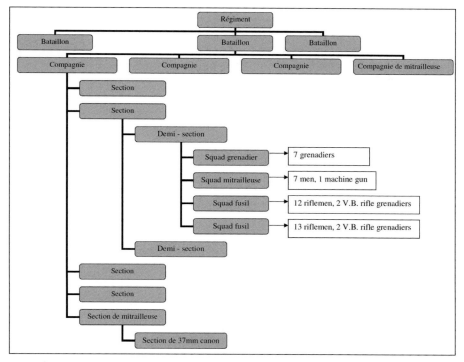

Organisation of a *Régiment d'infanterie*, April 1916.

The Infantry Division (*Division d'infanterie*)
1914

When France mobilised for war on 1ˢᵗ August 1914, the 'metropolitan' French Army consisted of forty four active divisions. Forty one of these were 'line' infantry divisions (numbered 1 to 36 and 39 to 43) and three were colonial (*1e, 2e,* and *3e Divisions d'infanterie coloniale*). Upon mobilisation, a further three divisions were formed - the *44e* (composed of four Alpine Infantry regiments), the *37e* and the *38e* – bringing the total number of active divisions at the war's commencement to forty seven.

Within three weeks, the *45e Division d'infanterie* and the *Division Marocaine* were formed in North Africa but, on 5ᵗʰ September 1914, the *44e Division d'infanterie* was dissolved. This same date, however, saw the formation of the *76e* and *77e Divisions d'infanterie,* boosting the numbers of active infantry divisions to forty nine (plus the 'non-metropolitan' *Division Marocaine*) by the end of of 1914.

In 1914, an infantry division was composed of two *brigades d'infanterie,* each comprising two *regiments d'infanterie* (each consisting of 3,000 soldiers, split between three *bataillons*). Three *Groupes d'artillerie* (each consisting of three *batteries de tir* of four 75mm guns), a cavalry squadron (*Escadron de cavalerie*) and a company of engineeres (*Compagnie de génie*) were also part of the divisional make-up, along with ancilliary services, such as the divisional Provost Company (*Compagnie de gendarmes*), a Medical Section (*Section de service de santé*), a Transport Squadron (*Escadron de Train des équipages*) and the Administration Section (*Section d'intendance*) were also attached. Some infantry divisions also had an attachment of one or two *Bataillons de chasseurs.* When at full strength, a *Division d'infanterie* would consist of approximately 16,000 soldiers, of whom over 85% would be infantrymen.

Two regiments of reserve infantry were also intended to be attached to each division but, upon mobilisation on 1 August, the majority of these were brought together and formed into twenty five independent reserve infantry divisions (the *51e* to the *75e Divisions d'infanterie*).

Four of these reserve divisions were assigned to the defence of fortified regions; the 57e *Division d'infanterie* was assigned to Belfort, the *71e* to Epinal, the *72e* to Verdun and the *73e* to Toul. The remaining twenty one became field formations. In September 1914, the *54e* and *75e* were dissolved, leaving twenty three reserve divisions by the end of the year.

The composition of a reserve infantry division differed to that of an 'active' infantry division in that it consisted of two *brigades,* each made up of three *régiments*. A reserve infantry regiment was smaller than an active infantry regiment, however, having only two *bataillons* (2,000 soldiers). Active and reserve infantry divisions were, therefore, both made up of twelve battalions each but, due to a lesser number of ancilliary troops, a reserve infantry division was slightly smaller overall in size, consisting of approximately 14,000 soldiers when at full strength.

1915

During 1915, reorganisations of divisions and inter-divisional regimental transfers eradicated the lack of uniformity between active and reserve infantry divisions. All active divisions (the few that had retained them) began to remove their attached reserve regiments and all reserve divisions became active. Extra ancilliary troops were added to each division and the *genie* were allocated to, and fell under the jurisdiction of, each *bataillon* as opposed to being under divisional control, as was the previous situation.

An increase in the size of the army due to the incorporation of the *Classe de 1915* in December 1914 and the *Classe de 1916* in April 1915, along with the incorporation of several unafilliated regiments, allowed for the formation of twenty six new divisions, including a further four *Divisions d'infanterie coloniale,* throughout the year. By the end of 1915, the French Army consisted of ninety eight active army *Divisions d'infanterie.*

1916

By 1916, the additional reserve regiments and *chasseur* groups attached to the active infantry divisions had been completely removed and amalgamated into their own seperate divisions. During other reorganisations, a trench artillery battery and a divisional infantry depot unit was added to each division; but the brigade system was dropped at the end of the year. An active *Division d'infanterie* would consist of three infantry regiments as its highest component, but would only be made up of approximately 13,000 soldiers at full strength. Due to this reorganisation, a further nine new divisions could be formed, making the number of active divisions by the end of the year 107.

The Territorial Division (*Division d'infanterie territoriale*)
1914

Numbered *81e* to *92e, 94e, 96e* and *97e,* there were fifteen *Divisions d'infanterie territoriale* in existence at the time of the August 1914 mobilisation. Mainly assigned to the coastal defences, Alpine border guard duties and the garrison of Paris, the *90e* and *94e Divisions* (amalgamated into the *94e* in September) had both been disbanded by October, with their regiments being distributed amongst the other divisions. Territorial divisions were independent of any particular *Corps d'armée* though, at various times, some divisions were brought together to form a divisional reserve group within a *Corps.*

A *Division d'infanterie territoriale* was composed of two *brigades* of two *régiments d'infanterie territoriale,* but the number of *bataillons* in a territorial regiment varied depending on the size of the population local to the area where the regiment was raised. The usual size of a regiment was three or four *bataillons* but, due to the variable nature of these units, there could be as many as seven or even as few as two. For this reason, a *Division d'infanterie territoriale,* though its component parts were similar, was generally far smaller than an active or reserve division. At full strength, a *Division d'infanterie territoriale* varied in size between 8,000 and 12,000 soldiers.

1915

Following on from the increase in the size of the army, the incorporation of non-allocated formations, and the call up into full time service of the *Classes* of 1892 in December 1914, 1891 in March 1915 and of 1890 and 1889 in April 1915 (all of whom were part of the *Réserve de l'armée territoriale* and nearing the end of their compulsory service commitments), it was possible to form a further six territorial divisions during 1915: the *99e* to the *101e* in February, the *102e* in May, and the *103e* to the *105e* in August. In June and July, however, seven territorial divisions (*82e, 84e, 85e, 86e, 91e, 92e* and the *96e*) were disbanded, with all of the regiments of the *85e* and *86e Divisions d'infanterie territoriale* being assigned to active army *Divisions d'infanterie*.

1916

Following the reorganisation of the divisional infantry and the dropping of the brigade structure within divisions, four territorial divisions were disbanded in 1916 (the *99e*, the *102e*, *103e* and *104e*). The *105e Division d'infanterie territoriale* also underwent a designation change in March 1916, becoming the *133e Division d'infanterie* of the active army. By the end of 1916 there were only seven territorial divisons still in existence.

Chapter Two

The Background:
The War 1914–1916

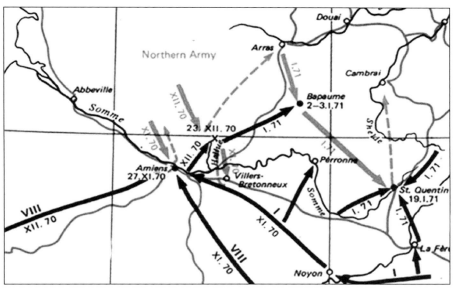

Movements of the German *1. Armee* and the French *Armée du Nord* in Picardy, November 1870 to January 1871.

No stranger to war across history, modern warfare first arrived in Picardy in November 1870, following which several actions of varying scale took place between General Edwin von Manteuffel's *1. Armee* and the French *Armée du Nord* under the command of *géneral* Charles Bourbaki and, later, *géneral* Louis Faidherbe. The first large scale battle in this area took place to the south and east of Amiens on 27 November, in which several villages that would become more famous just under half a century later were embroiled … Villers-Bretonneux, Marcelcave, Hangard and Cachy, to name just a few.

This battle was followed by others – Pont Noyelles/Hallue (23 -24 December 1870), Bapaume (2-3 January 1871) and St Quentin (19

11

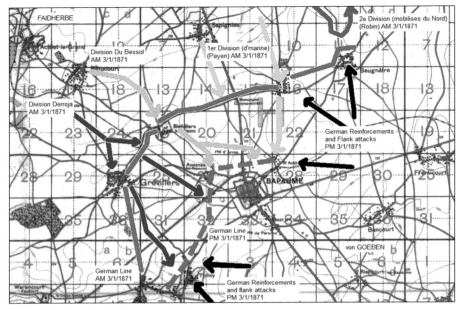

The *bataille de Bapaume*, 3 January 1871.

January 1871), all of which were fought over locations familiar to the student of the Great War. There was also the siege of Péronne (27 December 1870 – 10 January 1871), in which the Germans first realised the usefulness of La Maisonnette and Mont St Quentin for the positioning of artillery batteries – something that they would do again in 1914. It was a highly destructive siege and many of the villages around the town would also see some action, usually on a small scale, during this period as the Germans reinforced their positions and French soldiers and *francs tireurs* tried to disrupt them. Some locations that would be destroyed during the Great War also suffered serious damage during the late 1870-71 period as well; for example the village of Fay, badly hit during an artillery bombardment on the rear of the German siege positions. Following the conclusion of the 1870-71 Franco-German War, the area settled back into normality until the outbreak of the Great War in 1914.

1914 - The *batailles de Péronne, de Picardie* and *d'Albert*

Not part of the French war plans, the Somme was a very lightly defended area in August 1914. With the expectation that any German attack would come from the area of the Franco - German border, the invasion of Belgium and the use of that country as another entry point into France came as a surprise, although *géneral de division* Joseph Joffre, the *chef*

Memorial to *Marin* Delpas at Péronne. 21 year old Jean Delpas, from Lugas, Tarn, was serving with the *5e compagnie* of the *1e Bataillon de marine de marche* during the siege of Péronne when he was killed by a German shell detonating on the ramparts on 29 December 1870.

Memorial to the 3 January 1871 action at Bapaume. Located on the German northern defensive line at a point attacked by the *1e Division d'marine*, this monument is also the final resting place of a number of casualties from this battle.

d'État-Major des Armées (Chief of the Defence Staff**)**, suspected that this might occur and ordered an advance into southern Belgium on 14 August. After the Battles of Charleroi and Mons on 21 and 23 August 1914 and the general retreat that followed, it became apparent that Amiens was under threat from the German First Army as it pursued the British Expeditionary Force and the French *Ve Armée* back into France.

Lille was evacuated on 24 August and several thinly held defensive lines were formed to the north of the Somme. With the *61e* and *62e Divisions d'infanterie* being sent from Paris, just six divisions (plus 25,000 troops of the Lille garrison) held a 110 kilometer long line from Douai to Béthune and from Aire to the sea. On 25 August, the German II Corps advanced westwards to the vicinity of Cambrai, where, after being stopped temporarily in a holding action by French Territorials, they continued to advance the following day. *Groupe Ebener* were ordered to move to Combles and Péronne to become part of the *VIe Armée* but continued to retreat westwards, covered by the *84e Division d'infanterie territoriale*.

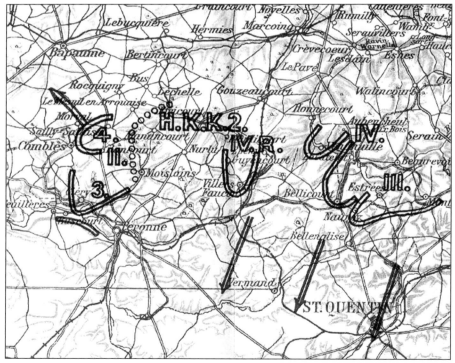

Situation in the evening of 27 August 1914 (*Der Weltkrieg 1914 bis 1918*).

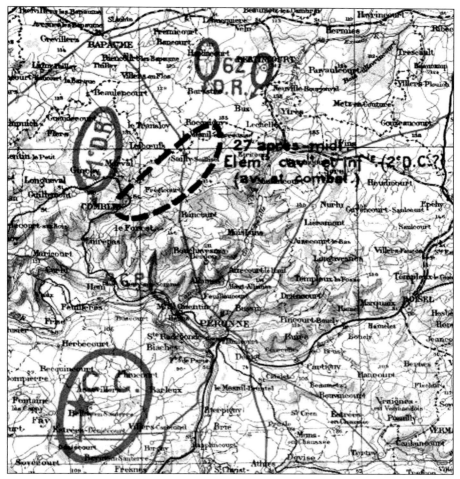

V Armée **Situation during the afternoon of 27 August 1914, as depicted in** *Les Armées Françaises dans la Grande Guerre.*

The Germans entered Péronne on 27 August 1914, following a brief cavalry action between Roisel and the eastern outskirts of the town and completely captured it the following day. On this same day, to the north, the *61e* and *62e Divisions d'infanterie* - elements of *Groupe d'Amade* – advanced in a south-easterly direction through Bapaume. In the area of Morval, Le Transloy, Sailly-Saillisel and Moislains, their path crossed with that of the German II Corps and an intense action (known as the Action of Mesnil and part of the *bataille de Péronne*) took place around this area that caused huge losses on both sides. The battle was joined by von der Marwitz's cavalry between Morval and Rancourt and the II Corps

15

advance, though delayed, continued. By 29 August, the advance had reached the line between Albert, Proyart and Chaulnes and, by the 30 August, had reached Amiens.

Held by the Germans for just under a fortnight, the German garrison at Amiens withdrew from the city on 11 September 1914, following on from reversals suffered at the Battle of the Marne and the general retreat of the German line. Precipitating the *1er bataille de Picardie*, the French advanced towards Fricourt and Péronne on 17 September in an attempt to outflank the Germans but were forced to halt as the Germans dug into defensive positions. To the south, the *VI Armée* had been frustrated at Carlepont and were forced to attack up the Oise River towards Noyon; whilst the *II Armée* on the Somme prepared to attack the northern flank of the German First Army.

Crossing the River Avre from Lassigny to Roye and Chaulnes, the *II Armée* stalled against the entrenched positions of the German II Corps who were reinforced by XVIII Corps, who soon pushed back the French *4e corps d'Armée* in the area of Roye. On 24 September, the French *II Armée* managed to secure a bridgehead on the east bank of the River Somme south of Péronne but, in doing so, exhausted their offensive capability – a situation taken advantage of the following day when a general German counter attack was launched across the Somme front.

Pushed back in the southern Somme sectors on 25 September, being forced back through Chaulnes and Soyécourt, the French *IIe Armée* managed an advance to the immediate south of Bapaume, but came under furious counter attack during what was to become known as the *bataille d'Albert*. By 26 September, following vicious fighting with the *II. Königlich Bayerisches Armee-Korps* around Le Transloy, Barastre, Lesboefs, Gueudecourt and Morval, before falling back towards the Somme River at Curlu and Maricourt, the French *11e Division d'infanterie*, the *82e, 84*e and *88e Divisions d'infanterie territoriale* and the *1e, 5e* and *10e Divisions de cavalerie* managed to establish a defensive line running north from Curlu, through Montauban, Longueval, Flers, Warlencourt and Achiet-le-Grand to Ervillers where, reinforced by the *21e* and *22e Divisions d'infanterie* (with the *19e Division d'infanterie* en route), it was hoped to make a stand and stop the German advance by 27 September.

Throughout 27 and 28 September, however, another German push was made towards Albert. The German *XIV. Reserve-Korps,* with the *II. Königlich Bayerisches Armee-Korps* to its south, advanced straight down and either side of the Bapaume-Albert road, coming into contact with *21e* and *22e Divisions d'infanterie* and the *88e Division d'infanterie territoriale* in such locations as Courcelette, Thiepval, Ovillers, La

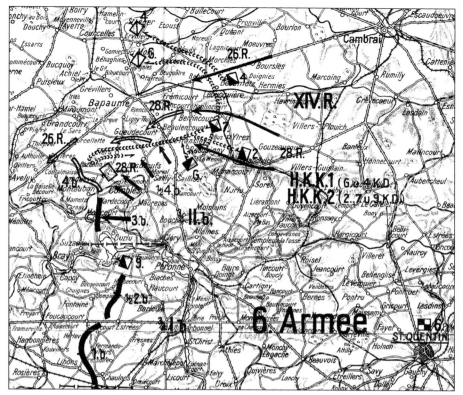

Movements of the German *6. Armee* during the *bataille d'Albert* 26 – 27 September 1914. The conclusion of this action would define the front lines on the Somme for the next two years. (*Der Weltkrieg 1914 bis 1918*).

Boisselle (where a particularly vicious fight for the village ensued), Fricourt and Mametz. A counter-attack by the *22e Division d'infanterie* on 28 September managed to break through as far as Courcelette but, after this counter attack was stopped, the surviving Frenchmen returned to Authuille Wood and Aveluy. The positions being held at this point were consolidated to prevent any further German advance. With the Germans digging in opposite, the line now became established from Hébuterne in the north, through Auchonvillers, towards Thiepval, opposite Ovillers, swinging eastwards at La Boisselle, opposite Fricourt, Mametz, down to Maricourt and then to the river Somme at Fargny, near Curlu.

South of the river, things had been a little more static over the previous few days. Although there was fighting around Dompierre, Fay, Estrées, Soyécourt, Vermandovillers and Lihons, positional warfare had set in and advances of anything more than a few metres by either side was almost impossible.

17

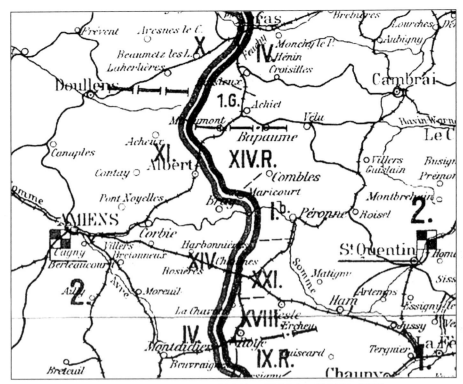

The Somme Front, 14 November 1914 (*Der Weltkrieg 1914 bis 1918*).

With the outflanking attempts by both sides taking place further to the north of the Somme through the remainder of September and into October, the front lines as they would remain, give or take a few hundred metres, until the 1916 Battle of the Somme in this sector began to be dug.

1914-15

Far from being the 'quiet backwater' front that many narratives of the Somme would have us believe, the Somme battlefield of 1914-15 was actually a very active front.

Though of no particular local strategic value, it was believed necessary to maintain some sort of aggressive attitude towards the enemy on the Somme throughout the remainder of 1914 as part of a general plan to keep German reserves in the west, thereby assisting the Russian allies on the eastern front. Though October was mainly spent in establishing the new lines, a few local operations intended to gain locally advantageous positions were carried out in locations such as Beaumont-Hamel and Ovillers. November and, especially, December, however, saw

18

these local operations step up a gear, with multi-battalion sized raids and small scale local offensives all along the Somme front – mostly with very limited, but costly, results. On 10 December 1914, a *28e Division d'infanterie* attack near Fay, south of the river, stalled on the German wire before the village with heavy French losses. This was followed a week later by an identical attack with identical results. At Hardecourt-aux-Bois, north of the river, a similar event and with similar results occurred on 17 December. That day actually witnessed a number of such attacks: at Beaumont-Hamel, Ovillers, La Boisselle, Mametz, Maricourt, Dompierre, Fay and Lihons – un-coordinated local offensives, unrelated to each other, all of which gained absolutely nothing other than inflicting a few casualties (but sustaining considerably more) and was typical of events on this front at this time. The only major territorial gain during these attacks took place at La Boisselle, where the French moved their front line forwards - placing the village cemetery and the *îlot* position into the front line and effectively narrowing No Man's Land rather than pushing the Germans back.

Christmas 1914 did not see many occasions of fraternisation on the Somme front, but rather a continuation of the December 'offensives'. A large scale raid took place at Ovillers on Christmas Eve and, at La Boisselle, there was fighting at the *îlot*. The first of the mine shafts preceding the underground war in this area was also sunk on this day and the village was heavily shelled. Raids took place between Fricourt and Mametz and, on the evening of Christmas Day, French engineers detonated a mine – the first of many – at Dompierre. The most significant action of Christmas 1914, however, was the three day long fight for the *briqueterie* position and *Côte 101* at Lihons where, following a German attack on Christmas Eve, a divisional sized retaliatory attack was conducted by the *27e Division d'infanterie* that by Boxing Day had extended to Vermandovillers.

1915 was a year of raids for the French Army on the Somme rather than all out attacks (other than one), as underground warfare dominated the sectors for the first half of the year. Intense mine warfare took place on Redan Ridge near Beaumont Hamel and to the north of Carnoy; but the No Man's Land at Frise, Dompierre and Fay (and, as intense, but over a smaller area, the *îlot* at La Boisselle) became a figurative moonscape of craters as hundreds of mines and camouflets were detonated over the first six months of the year.

The most significant attack of the year on the Somme battlefield (though, technically, it was and is in the Pas-de-Calais) was the *bataille d'Hébuterne,* which took place between the 7 and 13 June 1915. A diversionary attack and subsidiary action for the Second Battle of Artois,

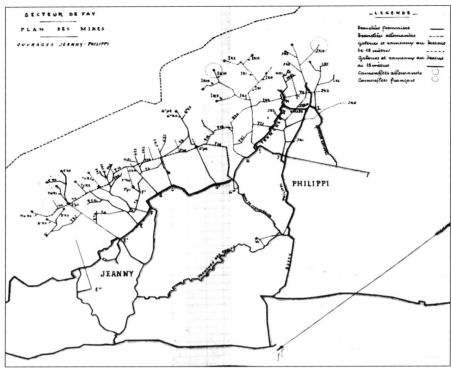

Mines Diagram, Fay Sector, December 1915.

regiments from the *21e, 27e, 51e* and *56e Divisions d'infanterie* (the *64e, 93e* and *137e Régiments d'infanterie* being the units taking part in the initial assault) carried out the advance along a 1,200 metre front and managed to capture Toutvent Ferme (a heavily fortified farm and strongpoint just behind the German front line and at the head of a small salient in the German line) and two lines of German defences between the villages of Hébuterne and Serre. Managing an advance of up to a kilometre in depth and moving the front line to the positions from which the 'Pals' Battalions of the (British) 31st Division would attack the following July, French losses amounted to over 1,700 dead and 8,500 wounded.

At the end of July 1915, and into August, the British Third Army began to relieve the parts of the French *II Armée* north of the river Somme. Holding the line from Ransart (south of Arras) to Curlu on the Somme River, the British held line was extended to the south of the river between Frise and Foucaucourt after the arrival of the XII Corps in

September 1915 (though 14 Brigade, 5th Division, had been located at Frise for a short while in August). Relieving the *154e Division d'infanterie* between 21 and 22 September 1915, the 26th, 22nd and 27th Divisions (north to south) held the south Somme sector for a month until the *6e Division d'infanterie*, almost directly from being in action during the Third Battle of Artois, replaced them on 22nd October 1915. Following this relief, these British divisions were despatched to Salonika.

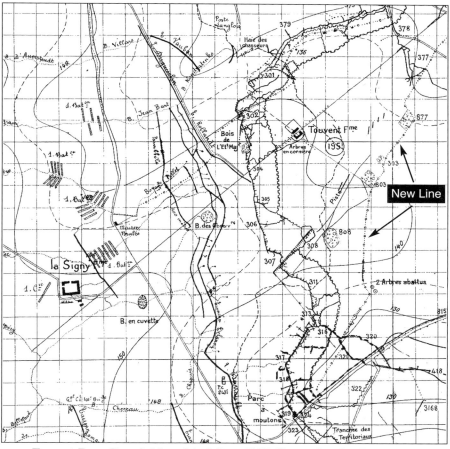

Touvent Farm Trench Map, 6 to 8 June 1915, illustrating the French and German trenches prior to and (dashed line) post the initial assault. A further slight advance in this area would form the front line from which the 'Pals' battalions of the British 31st Division would attack on 1 July 1916.

1916

On 28 January 1916, as part of a diversionary assault for the forthcoming offensive at Verdun, the German 11th Infantry Division launched an attack on the French *5e Division d'infanterie* at Frise. Attacking the village from the area of the canal to the north and also from the area of Herbecourt before sweeping northwards to attack and capture the southern section of the village, the front line was pushed back to within a kilometre of the French *9e Brigade* (*74e* and *274e Régiments d'infanterie*) headquarters, placing the Maricourt area north of the river and the Somme crossing at Eclusier at risk. French artillery, supported by the British artillery north of the river, began a huge bombardment on the German positions and a French counter-attack regained much of the lost territory between 2 and 3 February 1916. The village of Frise, however, remained in German hands.

Other than the actions at Frise, the remaining weeks of the first half of 1916 were given to trench holding and preparations for the forthcoming offensive.

Chapter Three

The Battle of the Somme
1916

Background to the Offensive

Originally conceived as part of a war-winning simultaneous strike on three fronts by all Allied nations, initial planning for what was to eventually become the Battle of the Somme began soon after the Italian declaration of war and as early as June 1915, when it was proposed by the French Commander-in-Chief, *général* Joseph Joffre, that the Allies (France, Russia, Great Britain, Serbia, Belgium and Italy) should begin to operate more co-operatively with each other and co-ordinate their plans accordingly. This proposal was taken up on 7 July 1915 when the first Inter-Allied Military Conference at Chantilly, Oise (the location of Joffre's *Grand Quartier Général*) was held. Though no specific actions were decided upon at this conference, it was agreed that concentrated, co-operative actions would be the most successful way forward and the foundations were laid for a second, more proactive, conference to be held later that year.

Following on from a meeting in Paris between the British Prime Minister, Herbert Asquith, and his French counterpart, Aristide Briand, on 17 November 1915, an agreement was made and adopted to form a permanent committee co-ordinating action between the two nations. A further Anglo-French meeting was held in Calais on 4 December 1915, presided over by Lord Kitchener, with the French delegation represented by Briand. Two days later, a second Chantilly Conference was held in which the Allied strategy for 1916 was to be decided. Here it was agreed that offensives by the Allied armies on the War Fronts should be delivered simultaneously or, at least, close enough in time to each other (within a month) so that the enemy would be prevented from being able to transport reinforcements from one front to another. These offensives were planned to commence as soon as was possible, with local, limited attacks taking place in between to further incapacitate and occupy the enemy forces.

On 29 December 1915 another meeting was called at Chantilly by Joffre, attended by the French President Raymond Poincaré, Prime Minister Aristide Briand, Minister of War *général* Gallieni and *générals* Dubail, de Langle de Cary and Foch; with the British representation being led by the newly appointed Commander in Chief, General Douglas Haig. Here Joffre persuaded Haig to use the B.E.F. to relieve the French *Xe Armée* between Arras and the Somme and suggested a look at the possibilities of a combined Franco-British offensive over a sixty mile front either side of the River Somme. He had ordered Foch to prepare an offensive from the River Somme southwards to Lassigny, informing Haig that a French offensive would be greatly aided by a simultaneous offensive of the British forces between the Somme and Arras, arguing that it would be advantageous to attack an enemy on a front where minimal activity had taken place for quite a while.

By 20 January 1916, Joffre revealed that he would have five offensives prepared by the end of April 1916 : three in Alsace-Lorraine, one on the Champagne Front and one, the previously discussed offensive, on the Oise-Somme front. Whichever was selected would depend on the specific situation at that particular time but, in the meantime, it would be important to wear the Germans down as much as possible. Consequently, Joffre suggested that the British should attack to the north of the River Somme on a minimum of a seven mile front around 20 April 1916. With no strategic importance, this was to form part of Joffre's *bataille d'usure*-intended simply to cause damage and soften up the enemy prior to a major – French led – offensive.

Haig, however, could not agree to this plan as, other than being politically unacceptable, his forces would not be ready by April and considered alternative plans for the remainder of the month.

Joffre abandoned this plan on 14 February 1916 after further discussions and it was agreed that a combined Franco-British offensive should be carried out on the Somme towards the end of June, with a smaller, solely British, attack being simultaneously launched between La Bassée and Ypres. A Corps from the French *VIe Armée* would also be placed immediately north of the River Somme to act as flank protection to the larger French forces attacking to the south.

However, on 21 February 1916, the Germans struck first. Launching their own offensive at Verdun on this date, it soon became clear that this battle was to become a long, drawn out battle of attrition in which much of the French Army on the Western Front would become committed. Joffre pressed Haig to continue with the relief of the *Xe Armée*, enabling the release of French reserves and, in March, requested that he do all that he could in harassing the enemy to prevent German reserves from reinforcing the Verdun front. He also requested that the preparations for the attack on the Somme should continue unabated. The plan was now for a combined attack between Hébuterne in the north and Lassigny in the south, but with, possibly, an earlier date than anticipated.

By the end of April 1916, due to the French situation at Verdun, it was beginning to look like the proposed Somme operation might have to be cancelled and that all offensive operations for the year might have to be passed on to the British. In May it seemed that any Somme offensive might have to be made without any French assistance at all and it became apparent that simultaneous Allied attacks utilising maximum force in a war-winning move was no longer possible.

However, following a meeting at Saleux on 31ˢᵗ May 1916 attended by Haig, Joffre, Briand, Foch, Poincaré, *général* de Castelnau and the new French Minister for War, *général* Pierre Roques, Haig stated that all he needed was a date to begin offensive operations on the Somme. Joffre then gave an assurance that, no matter what the situation at Verdun, he would have French Army assistance.

On 3 June 1916, Joffre gave formal notice that the date of the attack should be 1 July but, just ten days later, and due to a critical turn in events at Verdun, requested that the date be brought forward to 25 June. After a review of the situation, Haig reported back to Joffre that the B.E.F. could not begin the offensive at any time before 29 June. Joffre agreed and the date was set. As fate would have it, however, bad weather would force the date back to the originally agreed date of 1 July 1916 in any case.

The Preparations for 1ˢᵗ July 1916

Principally, the initial British role was simply to attempt to relieve pressure on Verdun and inflict losses on the enemy (though, by the time of the start of the offensive, the first of these aims had, in fact already been achieved by the Russian Army following the launch of the Brusilov Offensive on 4 June, which forced the Germans to call a halt to the attacks on Verdun and immediately transfer four infantry divisions to the Eastern Front to assist the Austro-Hungarian Army that had borne the brunt of the Russian attack). The French role at this stage, along with assisting the British in their task, was simply to guard the right flank of the main British attack and follow their advance on either side of the River Somme as the line was moved eastwards over a broad front, drawing in as many German reserves as possible. Hemmed in by the ninety degree bend in the River Somme to the south of Péronne, it was expected that this would limit any advance south of the river. However, it was known that the capture of the high ground to the north and south of the town would be extremely beneficial for any future offensive plans. It was with these basic tasks in mind that the preparations for battle were conducted.

North of the River Somme, General Haig committed the Fourth Army (under General Henry Rawlinson) to the offensive, with the Reserve Army (Lieutenant General Hubert Gough) in reserve and elements of the

Tirailleurs Sénégalais of the *Division Marocaine* marching through Boves, near Amiens, on 21 June 1916. In reserve on the opening day of the Battle of the Somme, these men would make a name for themselves over the following weeks on the Flaucourt Plateau, Biaches and at La Maisonnette.

Third Army (General Edmund Allenby) to take part in a diversionary action in the Gommecourt salient immediately to the north. The French committed, from *général* Ferdinand Foch's *groupe d'armées Nord*, the *VIe Armée* (under the command of *général de division* Marie Émile Fayolle) and the *Xe Armée* (*général de division* Joseph Alfred Micheler) in reserve.

Fayolle deployed the *20e Corps d'armée* (the highly reputable *corps de fer*, the Iron Corps) under *général de division* Maurice Balfourier on the northern bank of the river, giving protection to both the right flank of the British attack and the left flank of the French. To the south was the *1e Corps d'armée colonial* (*général de division* Pierre Berdoulat) and *35e Corps d'armée* (*général de division* Charles Jacquot). A fourth corps, *2e Corps d'armée* (*général de division* Denis Auguste Duchêne) was held in reserve. Including the subsidiary action at Gommecourt, the British committed fourteen divisions to the first wave on the first day of the assault, the French committed six - with a further five playing a subsidiary role. By the end of the battle this involvement had been evened up – fifty-one British and Dominion divisions took part in the Somme battle compared to forty-eight French.

On 24 June 1916, the artillery preparation began. With 732 heavy guns and howitzers and a similar number of smaller calibre, plus over

Général de division **Maurice Balfourier, commander of the** *20ᵉ corps d'armée,* **in conversation with the President of France, Raymond Poincaré, at his headquarters at Méricourt sur Somme on 16 July 1916. Note the disinterested looking commander in chief,** *Général* **Joseph Joffre, wandering away to the right.**

1,100 trench-mortars (with over six million 75mm, and two million heavier rounds available) at the disposal of the *VIe Armée*, concentrating on a length of front line only fourteen kilometres long over the next six days, the bombardment of high explosives, shrapnel and gas was horrific for the German defenders. Highly experienced in the current tactics of artillery through many months of high intensity combat, the majority of the French gunners involved were veterans of the Battles of Artois and Champagne and many of those serving with the *20e Corps d'armée* north of the river had only recently arrived from one of the most intense artillery battles in history – Verdun. Combined with no real shortcomings in ammunition - either in quantity or quality – the French preliminary bombardment, unlike that of their British counterparts, was highly successful.

Behind the front line, the French improved the road networks and constructed light railways to assist in the forward movement of troops and supplies, bridges were constructed and repaired, accommodations

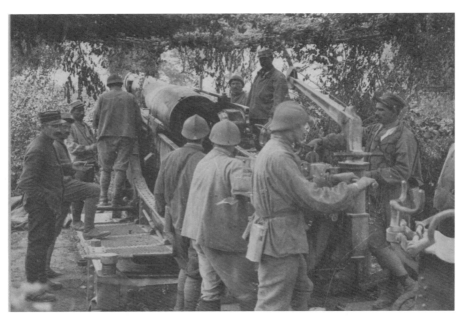

A French artillery team loading a *Mortier de 280 mle 1914 Schneider* siege howitzer near Cappy on 28 June 1916 during the preliminary bombardment for the Battle of the Somme.

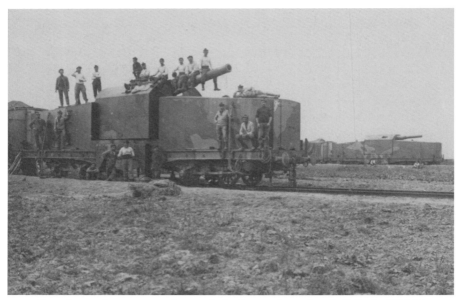

French naval gunners posing on their *Canon de marine de 274 mle 1893/96* railway gun near Rosiéres en Santerre, June 1916.

improved and supply depots set up. French engineers worked tirelessly up to and beyond (and under) the front lines. Patrol activity was increased, with nightly assessments of damage and intelligence reports written during any lull in the bombardment. All this activity could not and did not go unnoticed by the Germans but, believing the French to be totally worn down by the actions at Verdun and incapable of any offensive action, German intelligence reported all this as simply a ruse to divert reserves away from the expected attack north of the river and, therefore, of no threat.

220mm ammunition in transit to the firing line.

The First Day
Still making full use of artillery during the actual assault of 1 July 1916, the French fire plan was intended to destroy the first lines, enable registration on the second lines and to support the advancing infantry with a precisely regulated forward moving barrage. Objectives were individually selected with regard to their influence on the next phase of the battle (as opposed to the British idea of a 'general advance') and artillery preparations were used to neutralise positions for the infantry to

29

Heavy artillery ammunition of various calibres after being offloaded at the
gare de ravitaillement **at Marcelcave, 27 June 1916.**

Forward Observation Officer of the artillery directing fire in the region of
Estrées.

Schneider *Mortiers de 320 Mle 1870/93*
railway guns of the *artillerie lourde à*
grande puissance in action during the
preliminary bombardments at the end
of June 1916.

simply occupy and hold. Trench artillery, used in batteries, constantly pummelled the German front line positions, whilst locations deep within the defensive system were hit by shells of huge calibre from the guns of the *Artillerie Lourde à Grande Puissance* located in the French rear. Co-ordination between reconaissance aircraft of the *Service Aéronautique*, forward observers on the ground and the batteries in the rear ensured that up to the minute information and targetting were available. Even the cartographers of the *Groupes de Canevas de tir des Armées* were able to update the accuracy of trench maps (mainly by alteration of existing maps) due to this effective and rapid communication.

Moving forward in small groups, utilising any available cover, the infantry advanced using the fire and manoeuvre techniques learned the hard way since the days of the Second Battle of Artois the previous spring. Lightly encumbered initial waves followed the creeping barrage over the shattered German defences, followed in turn by grenadiers and other *Nettoyeurs de Tranchées* (literally translated as 'trench mopper-uppers' or 'trench cleaners') and then the next waves - equipped with the tools required to consolidate and hold the newly conquered positions. All contributed to an extremely successful first day of battle in which all objectives (and, in some cases, beyond) were taken other than for a small section of Bois

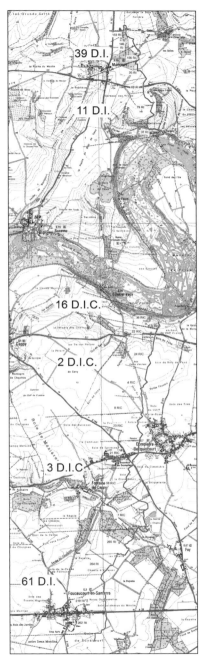

The French front line on the Somme battlefield of 1 July 1916.

31

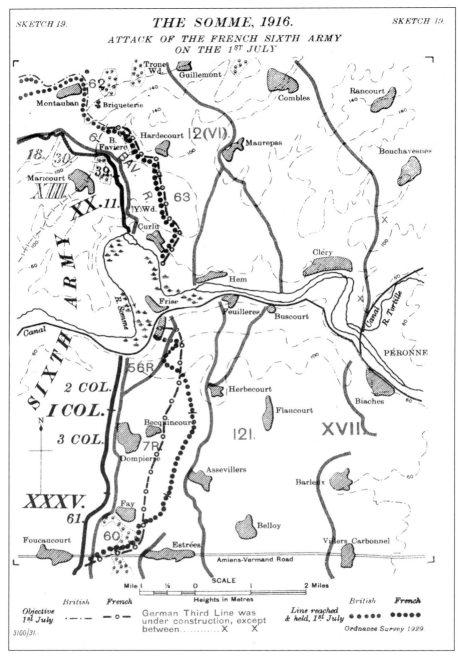

THE SOMME, 1916.

ATTACK OF THE FRENCH SIXTH ARMY
ON THE 1ST JULY

Trones Wd.
Guillemont
Combles
Rancourt
Montauban
Briqueterie
Hardecourt
Maurepas
Bouchavesnes
B. Favière
Maricourt
Curlu
Y.Wd.
Cléry
Hem
Frise
Feuillères
Buscourt
PÉRONNE
Canal
R. Somme
Canal
R. Tortille
Herbecourt
Flaucourt
Biaches
Becquincourt
Dompierre
Assevillers
Barleux
Fay
Belloy
Foucaucourt
Estrées
Villers Carbonnel
Amiens-Vermand Road

SCALE
Mile ½   O   2 Miles
Heights in Metres

British   French   British   French
Objective   German Third Line was   Line reached
1st July   under construction, except   & held, 1st July
                  between.......... X   X
3100/31.   Ordnance Survey 1929.

VI Armeé Attack, 1 July 1916. (British Official History)

French shells hitting the German line to the north of Dompierre.

Favière, next to the British sector north of the river, and the village of Frise to the south.

20e Corps d'armée sector (north of the river)

Located on the three kilometres of front line from the junction with the British 30th Division at Maricourt down to the River Somme at Fargny, the *39e* and *11e Divisions d'infanterie* (*général* Adolphe Guillaumat and *général* Eugène François Germain Vuillemot respectively) were the two divisions making up the first wave of the attack on 1 July 1916. Both were highly experienced divisions, made up of veterans of the Second Battle of Artois, the Second Battle of Champagne and, most recently, Verdun, where, throughout March and April 1916, they had been heavily engaged in the area of Douaumont and Vaux. Some of the older soldiers were even survivors of the murderous Battles of the Frontiers and had served in this area previously during the First Battle of Picardy in September 1914 before taking part in the First Battle of Ypres. Having lost heavily throughout 1914 and 1915, even many of the 19 and 20 year old reinforcements of the *Classe de 1916* were veterans of the mincing machine of Verdun. By July 1916, a few of the 19 year olds who made up the older end of the *Classe de 1917* had begun to filter through, the Somme becoming their first action. They would, however, be well educated in the art of war as members of such experienced units.

Launching their assault in conjunction with the British at 7.30am on 1 July 1916, as a testament to the highly effective French artillery, the two divisions advanced over the demolished German defences and

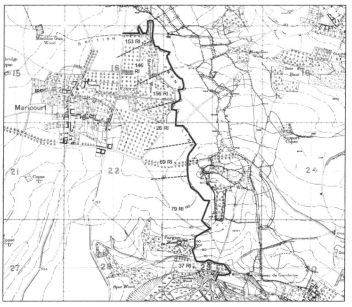

French Regiments North of the Somme, 1 July 1916.

Attack of the *39e* and *11e Divisions d'infanterie*, 1 July 1916 (Regimental Order).

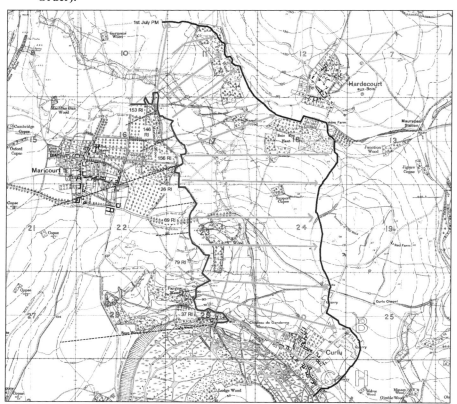

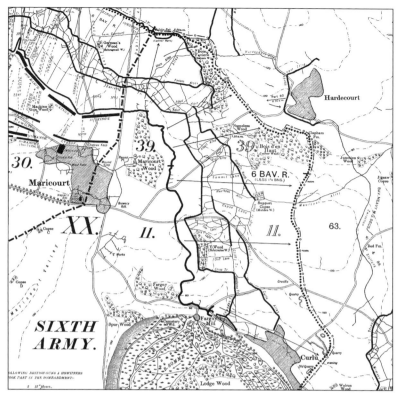

Attack of the *39e* and *11e Divisions d'infanterie*, 1 July 1916 (British Official History).

destroyed barbed wire entanglements relatively unimpeded (one first wave regiment – the *69e Régiment d'infanterie* of the *11e Division d'infanterie,* advancing either side of the Albert-Péronne road – even 'suffered' from zero fatalities and just fifteen wounded on the first day). Only at the extreme north and south of the *20e Corps* attack was there any hold up.

By 12.30pm, the *39e Division d'infanterie* had attained nearly all of its first day objectives - the German first line, Bois d'en Haut, Bois Sans Nom and Bois Favière, falling short by just seventy metres in the north-east corner of Bois Favière following some intense hand-to-hand combat in the remains of the trees. This small section would remain unconquered for another week.

To the south of the *39e Division d'infanterie*, *général* Vuillemot's *11e Division d'infanterie* advanced just as rapidly across the open plaine de Curlu, capturing Bois de l'Endurance with little opposition. South of the

35

French and British soldiers jointly engaged in road repairs at Maricourt.

The cleaning of squad mess equipment ('*marmites collective*' or '*Bouthéons*') in the River Somme at the remains of the mill at Fargny. Note the white cliff face of the *chapeau de gendarme* in the background. It was over this area that *37e Régiment d'infanterie* attacked on 1 July.

Albert-Péronne road, the fortified bastion of Bois Y was practically walked through by the *79e Régiment d'infanterie* and, aided by the concealing properties of the early morning river mist, the Hardecourt valley was crossed with ease. The fortified village of Curlu was entered mid-morning by the *37e Régiment d'infanterie*; but here the advance was held up by machine guns and defences located within the cellars and buildings of the village and in the surrounding phosphate quarries that had provided some cover from the intense preliminary bombardment. A violent bombardment was called in, pinpointing the German points of resistance, during the afternoon and the attack recommenced at 6pm. By 7pm the village and, therefore, the southernmost objective north of the river, was largely in French hands.

The village of Curlu after the battle.

During the afternoon, *Général* Balfourier had urged the British XIII Corps to continue their advance to the northwest of *20e Corps* in order to give flank protection to the French and allow them to continue the advance beyond the objectives. This request had been denied and, as it would have been folly to advance further without flank protection from the British, the line from Curlu in the south to Bois Favière in the north was consolidated and held against several German counter-attacks throughout the remainder of the day and into the night.

1e Corps d'armée coloniale and *35e Corps d'armée* sectors (south of the river)

South of the river, the *1e Corps d'armée colonial* and *35e Corps d'armée* were scheduled to launch their attack at 9.30am - two hours later than

German dead in the ruins of Curlu, 2 July 1916.

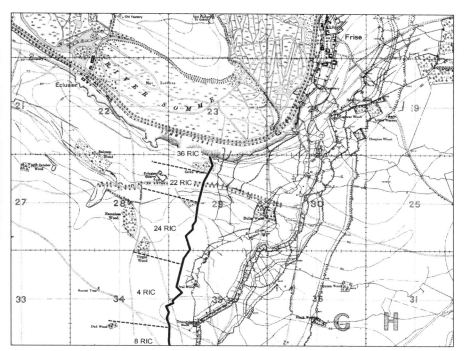

Regimental Order South of the Somme (River to North of Dompierre).

the assault to the north; it added to the belief that the southern attack was simply a ruse to draw reserves away from the north. In this area, between the southern bank of the Somme opposite Frise to the Roman road between Amiens and St Quentin, the preparatory bombardment had been more effective than anywhere else on the Allied Somme front and had managed effectively to silence the German artillery batteries in the area and forced the defenders into isolated machine gun positions and small groups of infantry manning shattered trenches and shell holes but, more often than not, driven them into the open. Penetrating the many weak spots, the French attackers, unhurried in their actions, manoeuvred around centres of resistance to cut them off and neutralise them from all angles. By the end of the day all objectives (apart from Frise, located in a particularly difficult position bordering the river and the Somme marshes) had been taken, the German Second Line approached in preparation for further attack and over 3,000 German prisoners captured.

At the northernmost point of the *1e Corps d'armée coloniale* area a single regiment, the *36e Régiment d'infanterie coloniale*, representing the *16e Division d'infanterie coloniale* (under the command of *général de division* Gaëtan Bonnier), had been given the unenviable task of

39

A pre-war view of Frise.

Frise after its capture on 2 July 1916. Note the German sign barring the use of the road due to the fact that it was in view of the enemy.

A shell damaged lock on the Somme Canal near Frise, July 1916.

advancing eastwards and then sweeping northwards along the Somme canal and capturing most of the village of Frise (fortified by the French between September 1914 and January 1916, but 'reversed' and re-fortified by the Germans since that latter date) along with three wooded areas and, if possible, continuing into the heavily defended Bois de Méraucourt. Though the artillery bombardment had smashed the German first lines here, facilitating an easy advance from their start positions around the Bois de la Vache and had also neutralised many of the defences before and within the Bois de Méraucourt, it had been less effective in the marshland north of the canal. Although hit by artillery from both north and south of the river over the past week, the formidable German machine gun and observation positions at La Grenouillére in the marshes north of Frise remained fully functional and relatively undamaged. Upon sweeping northwards after the capture of the German first lines, the *36e Régiment d'infanterie coloniale* came under extremely heavy fire from this position, being delayed there long enough for the Germans to reinforce and reorganise in the village of Frise. Pushing as far as the village cemetery, the French advance met with a German defence that was so tenacious that it proved impossible to advance any further into the village on this day and it became one of only two French opening day objectives not to be attained.

South of the *16e Division d'infanterie coloniale*, the *2e Division d'infanterie coloniale* (*général de division* Emile Alexis Mazillier) had a simpler, though no less important, task: to advance down the Cappy – Herbécourt road and across the open plain towards Herbécourt, in the process crossing the old (pre January 1916) French front line and the first four lines of trenches that made up the old German first line positions. Heavily enclosed by thick belts of barbed wire and defended by countless defensive positions interspaced with deep shelters, this area would have been almost impossible to penetrate prior to the preliminary bombardment. However, in an almost text book demonstration of the power of artillery, the area had been totally devastated and, other than for a few pockets of resistance, the German defence had been obliterated, enabling the French to advance across the smashed trenches and caved-in shelters with very light opposition. Upon reaching their final objectives – a line running north to south before and between Herbécourt and Assevillers, however, several units came under heavy machine gun fire from the village and the advance was halted for the evening.

The *3e Division d'infanterie coloniale* south of here (under the command of *général de division* Maurice Puypéroux who, though not officially in command until 2 July, directed operations following the severe wounding by shellfire of *général de division* Henri Gadel on 28

41

Dompierre during the afternoon of 1 July 1916. A lightly wounded *soldat colonial* is assisted to the rear by a soldier from an attached *section d'infirmiers militaires* as, in the background, a pair of *brancardiers* manoeuvre a wheeled stretcher towards the front line.

The ruins of Dompierre after its capture.

Troops from a *Régiment d'infanterie coloniale* of the *3e Division d'infanterie coloniale* rest in the ruins of Dompierre whist awaiting orders, 2 July 1916.

June 1916) had similar objectives to that of the *2e Division d'infanterie coloniale* but with one potential stumbling block. Part of their first objective was the heavily fortified 'twin' villages of Dompierre-Becquincourt, which had been held by the Germans since September 1914 and had been turned into a fortress over the preceding twenty one months of occupation. It had proven impossible to directly assault it previously, resulting in the occurrence of mine warfare throughout the middle of 1915 as the French attempted to dislodge the German front lines defending the villages and, so, was a worry to the French commanders given the task of advancing in this area. They need not have been concerned, however, as, following the preliminary bombardment (along with, according to the regimental history of the *22e Régiment d'infanterie coloniale*, the detonation of two mines and a 'false' attack), most of the German defences had been destroyed and, after capturing the German first lines within fifteen minutes, the villages fell with very little

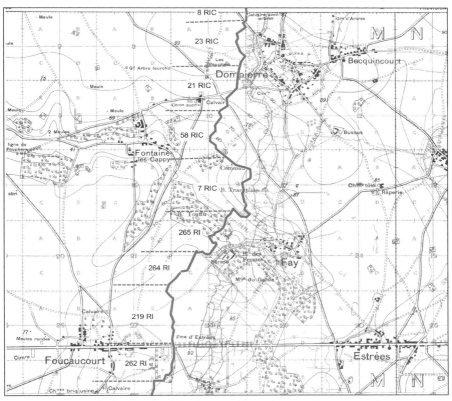

Regimental Order South of the Somme (Dompierre to Foucaucourt).

43

loss. Like their northern neighbours, the first day's attack stopped upon the capture of all objectives and in the face of heavy machine gun fire from the villages just beyond the objective.

Representing the *35e Corps d'armée* on the first day, the *61e Division d'infanterie* (*général de division* Charles Alexis Vandenberg) was tasked with the southernmost attack, between the Amiens – St Quentin road in front of Foucaucourt and the village of Fay. Its objectives were the section of heavily defended belt of woodland north of the road and the village of Fay whilst advancing into the German lines with no southerly flank protection. Potentially it had the most difficult task other than that given to the *36e Régiment d'infanterie coloniale* at Frise.

The ruins of the village of Fay, July 1916.

French artillerymen pose for a photograph outside the church of St Martin, Fay.

At Fay, in the northern part of the division's sector, once again the artillery had all but obliterated the German defences, enabling the advancing *264e and 265e Régiments d'infanterie* to advance through the village and surrounds with ease and to capture their second objective, the *Tranchée de Loge*, about a kilometer to the east. It was decided to call a halt to the advance here before the third objective – the defensive line south of Assevillers – was assaulted, to prevent the formation of a potentially difficult salient to defend was formed in the French line.

On the Amiens – St Quentin road, the final objective was to capture the eastern edge of Bois du Satyre and construct a south facing defensive line to protect the southern flank of the whole offensive. A formidable obstacle, the heavily entrenched Bois du Satyre had been hammered by the French heavy artillery prior to the attack and, immediately before it, bombarded with over 40,000 gas shells. Within ten minutes of the 9.30am launch of the attack, the western edge of the wood had been reached (following the familiar story of a simple walk over across the destroyed German front lines) and patrols were sent into the fallen trees to report back on the German situation. During the early afternoon, the wood was entered by two whole regiments and, though progress was slow and in some areas difficult due to isolated machine gun positions and heavy German artillery fire from the south, this being an area that was in range of German batteries that had not been knocked out by the French bombardment, the eastern fringe was attained and held by late afternoon.

Below the southernmost unit of the *61e Division d'infanterie* (the *262e Régiment d'infanterie*), south of the Amiens – St Quentin road, the *51e Division d'infanterie* (*general de division* Albert Boulange) held the area opposite Soyécourt and Vermandovillers. Not involved in a direct

Bois de Satyre and Bois de Soyècourt astride the Amiens -St Quentin road. The trench running the length of the road was the French front line between the end of 1 July and 4 July 1916.

assault on 1 July 1916, they gave fire support to the southern flank and, through an increase of aggressive patrol activity, kept the German defenders occupied in this sector throughout the day until the *61e Division d'infanterie* could construct effective southern flank defences.

Unlike in the British sectors, the first day of the Battle of the Somme ended, for the French, as a day of unprecedented success. Although they had just fallen short of attaining complete success so far as objectives were concerned on this day, they had managed to advance up to three kilometres and, in some locations, advanced beyond their objectives. Some units in the north were only prevented from advancing further due to British lack of progress further north. Over 4,000 German prisoners were captured by the French on 1 July, plus a considerable amount of *materiel*; and nowhere in the French sector was it deemed necessary to bring forward the reserves. Several counter-attacks were successfully

Convoys of German prisoners being moved to the rear, Dompierre sector 1 July 1916.

fought off overnight and, by midnight on 1 July, practically all of the French line was in the planned position, ready for the offensive to continue the following day.

Casualties for the French on 1 July were relatively light – the *VIe Armée* as a whole suffering some 1,590 casualties throughout the first day. However, the French blood-letting on the Somme was yet to come.

The First Fortnight... the continuation of the first phase of the Battle of the Somme
North of the River
Hindered by the British failures of 1st July and, less significantly, due to the congestion of units in the Maricourt-Curlu area complicating re-supply to the front, it was realised that moving the line forward in the *20e Corps d'armée* sector during the first week of the battle would have been extremely dangerous. Though they would have provided northerly protection for the advance south of the river, their own northerly flanks would have been dangerously exposed. Consideration was also given to the opinion that the Germans would rightly deem the junction between the French and British Armies to be a weak spot in the line and it was expected that this would become the focus of any major German counter-attack. Consolidation and strengthening of the newly gained line was, therefore, considered to be of primary importance in this area until the British were again in a position to advance.

Other than the almost continuous skirmishing in the north-eastern corner of Bois Faviére and the slight positional adjustments carried out on the north bank of the Somme in front of Curlu, the French line held by the *20e Corps d'armée* remained relatively stable between 2 and 4 July. On 5 July, due to German artillery fire coming from the Hem plateau and causing problems for the *1e Corps d'armée coloniale* south of the river, it became necessary for French operations to recommence north of the river. The heavily defended village of Hem was attacked during the morning and by the evening of 5 July was in French hands, along with most of the Hem plateau. Though this area would continue to be heavily fought over for the next week and with the Germans managing to regain a good proportion of the area lost on the 5th, the artillery that had been previously located there had been silenced. The advance then stalled - boxed in by the strong points of Monacu Ferme to the east and Bois de Hem to the north.

At the northern end of the French line, following on from several local British advances, the next attack was scheduled for 7 July. However, a strong German attack on Bois Faviére pre-empted this attack and resulted in the loss of parts of the northern section of the wood. Though recaptured

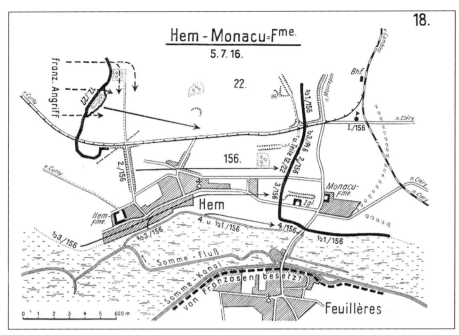

Hem 5 July 1916 (from *Schlachten des Weltkrieges*).

in an immediate counter-attack, the scheduled assault was delayed for twenty four hours and, as part of a combined Anglo-French attack (in conjunction with the British 30th Division attacking towards Maltz Horn Farm and Trônes Wood), the *39e Division d'infanterie* attacked the western slopes of Hardecourt Ridge and village. Under the cover of an intense bombardment, the approach to the village was swiftly covered; but it would take two hours of fierce hand to hand fighting both above and - in the cellars and tunnels dug below the village, interconnected with the catacombs of the church - below ground before the village was completely captured.

The French line north of the river now, once again, became static as the new line was consolidated in preparation for the next phase of the battle

South of the River

South of the Somme the successes of the first day were immediately followed up on the second day after intelligence reports were received regarding the withdrawal of German artillery positions from the Flaucourt Plateau. French artillery began by systematically destroying German wire and strongpoints in the unconquered sections of the German Second Line, leaving the defences weak and open to fresh French assaults. In the north of this sector, a fresh attack on Frise by the *36e Régiment d'infanterie coloniale* secured the village during the morning of 2 July and, following the German abandonment of the Grenouillère position in the marshes to the north, this advance along the southern bank of the Somme river continued unabated during the afternoon through to the eastern edge of the Bois de Méreaucourt, where the line was consolidated during that evening of 2 July.

To the immediate south of here, the village of Herbécourt was flanked by the *36e Régiment d'infanterie coloniale* and the *24e Régiment d'infanterie coloniale* before being directly occupied by the *22e Régiment d'infanterie coloniale*, who pushed through the village to set up a defensive perimeter on its eastern edge. Other than a small advance by the *3e Division d'infanterie coloniale* east of Dompierre and north of Assevillers during the afternoon (shortening the distance for a direct assault on Assevillers the next day), no other advances were made in this

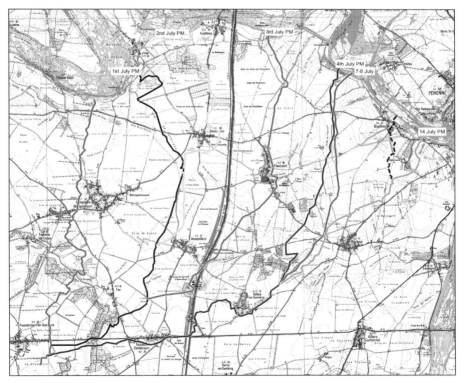

French Advances South of the Somme 1 – 15 July 1916.

Soldiers of the *22e Régiment d'infanterie coloniale* resting outside a shell damaged restaurant in Herbécourt following their capture of the village on 2 July 1916.

The ruins of Herbécourt church.

area as, by the end of this second day of battle, practically the whole of the German Second Line south of the river was in French hands.

The 3rd July saw the continuation of the general advance along the whole line over the open countryside of the Flaucourt Plateau, from the area to the south west of Assevillers up to the river Somme. Assevillers fell to the *3e Division d'infanterie coloniale* after a short fight by 9am, Flaucourt – practically abandoned by the Germans the previous night – fell to the same division by midday and Feuilléres became the next conquest of the *36e Régiment d'infanterie coloniale* of the *16e Division d'infanterie coloniale* at around the same time. The regiment then pushed on and captured the Bois du Chapitre and the hamlet of Buscourt and, therefore, the German 'secondary' defences that were intended to protect the Somme River crossings before the end of the day.

Feuilléres fell to the French of 3 July and later served as a launch point for an attack on Monacu Farm across the river.

The Second Line village of Assevillers.

By this point, *général* Fayolle was pressurised by Foch to continue the advance as quickly as possible and to exploit the successes south of the river, especially as the town of Péronne, the village of Biaches and (most importantly) the commanding heights of La Maisonnette were now all in view from the French frontline and, seemingly, easily achievable, given the disarray that the German defenders in the area appeared to be in. He was, however, reluctant to pursue an ill co-ordinated advance based on speculative intelligence. Far more important to him was the reorganisation of his units, the resupply of his forward troops and for the artillery, which had, so far, proved an essential element in the success, to be brought forward in line with the advance, thus preventing the enemy from being able to regain the initiative.

In line with Fayolle's orders, therefore, and preceding a general relief over 4 and 5 July, several units that had been in action since the opening day were finally relieved from action during the night of 3/4 July. The *Régiment de marche de la Légion étrangère* of the *Division Marocaine* replaced the *7e Régiment d'infanterie coloniale* from the *3e Division d'infanterie coloniale* in front of Assevillers and elements of the *53e Division d'infanterie* relieved units of the *61e Division d'infanterie* to their south. French artillery batteries also moved forward, taking up positions on the western edges of the Flaucourt Plateau and in front of Dompierre and Fay. During this same night, the German defenders began working frantically on strengthening their Third Line positions and attempted to link them, via Belloy-en-Santerre, to their, as yet unassaulted, Second Line positions at Estrées.

On 4 July, following a three hour bombardment, another general advance along the front was launched. In the south, the *329e Régiment d'infanterie* of the *53e Division d'infanterie* entered and captured the majority of the village of Estrées, thereby extending the southern flank of the whole offensive further along the Amiens – St Quentin road. Slightly to the west, the French front was also pushed southwards by 150 metres off the road and into the Bois de Soyécourt south of it in order to attempt to protect this flank. Severely fought over for the next two days, Estrées changed hands several times before the front was stabilised here, still without the whole village being captured, on the evening of 5 July. It would take until 24 July before the Germans were totally cleared from this village.

To the north of Estrées, the *Régiment de marche de la Légion étrangère* launched their costly, but ultimately successful, attack on Belloy-en-Santerre, which had been one of the very few failures in the French artillery preparations up to this point, forming a slight salient in the French line. This had to be desperately defended for the following

Trench relief: Colonial troops moving out of the line and passing the old German positions between Dompierre and Assevillers, 3 July 1916.

few days but would be successfully held until the French southerly extension of the offensive in September 1916. North east of Belloy, a cluster of woods: Grand Bois, Petit Bois, Bois Est and Bois Cheminée, proved to be an unattainable objective for the *21e Régiment d'infanterie coloniale* until the night of 4/5 July. They had been a camouflaged resupply point, invisible to the French gunners, and were the origin of several German counter-attacks on Belloy throughout the day.

Above here, a further 1,700 metres of the Flaucourt Plateau, including its highest points, was taken by the *2e Division d'infanterie coloniale* after over fourteen hours of constant combat and the line advanced to within 1,300 metres of Biaches. A prominent loop in the River Somme was by-passed, leaving the hamlet of Omiécourt-lès-Cléry in German hands until September.

Belloy en Santerre: yet another martyred Somme village.

During the night of 4/5 July, the *72e Division d'infanterie* entered the line immediately south of the river, holding the sector previously captured and fought over by the *36e Régiment d'infanterie coloniale*; the *16e Division d'infanterie coloniale* (minus the *36e Régiment d'infanterie coloniale,* who had been in action since 1st July) relieved the *2e Division d'infanterie coloniale* on the Flaucourt Plateau above Biaches; and the remainder of the *Division Marocaine* moved into the line around Belloy to replace the *3e Division d'infanterie coloniale.*

Harassed by artillery fire from the Hem Plateau north of the river (a problem solved by the localised actions in that vicinity from 5 July onwards), and now within range of the German guns at Mont St Quentin and easily observable from La Maisonnette, consolidation of the new positions took place over the next few days. As feared by Fayolle, the attack south of the river seemed to be losing momentum as the advance continued and logistics became stretched. With reports of reinforcements arriving to the German rear, it was an unfortunate necessity that it would be at this point that a pause in the advance (other than for a few localised actions to push the line forward a few metres into more advantageous positions and a failed assault on the village of Barleux on the 5th) was necessary to allow preparation for a further concerted effort on the German Third Line between Biaches and Barleux.

Originally scheduled for 8 July, wet weather forced a twenty four hour postponement to the next general attack south of the Somme. Following an intensive, thirty hour long, bombardment, the attack was launched on

The centre of the village of Biaches in August 1916. The junction of the rue de Péronne and the rue de Barleux, this marked the French front line at the end of the battle.

French communication trench on the rue du Moulin, Biaches.

9 July with much of the heavily defended village of Biaches falling to the *72e Division d'infanterie* during the evening of the first day and the remainder being captured on the 10th. To their south, the *16e Division d'infanterie coloniale* managed to wrest control of La Maisonnette from the Germans but sustained huge losses in the process and lost it the following day, being pushed back to its western slope. This began a struggle for this dominating position which was taken and lost at least nine times before the French finally gave up trying to hold on to it on 29 October 1916.

By 14 July, the eastern edge of Bois Blaise had been captured by the French, just one kilometer from the Somme crossing at Péronne, but a succession of furious German counter-attacks on 15 and 17 July pushed the line back to the west of the village of Biaches. A French attack on 19 July managed to recapture about half of the village and it would be in this unsatisfactory position that the line would remain until the end of the Battle of the Somme.

South of the Biaches – La Maisonnette areas, the *16e Division d'infanterie coloniale* once again found Barleux to be unattainable. Surrounded by hidden machine gun positions and dominated by high ground on three sides, the village remained in German hands. From

The chateau of La Maisonnette as it looked in 1913.

The ruins of the chateau of La Maisonnette following the German withdrawal in 1917.

The sugar factory in Biaches – a French front line position from mid-July 1916 through to the end of the Battle of the Somme.

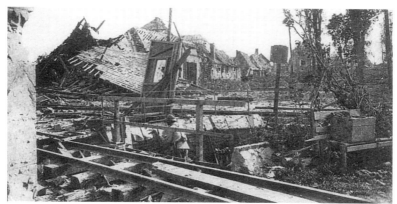

The junction of the rue de Péronne and the rue de Barleux in Biaches, (This photograph was taken from almost exactly opposite the earlier image of this location – note the reverse of the small directional sign visible just to the right of centre).

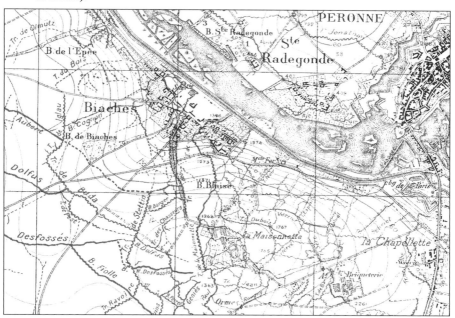

Biaches - La Maisonnette Trench Map, August 1916.

Barleux up to Biaches, dominated by the unconquerable La Maisonnette and boxed in by the River Somme to the north and to the east, despite some of the bitterest fighting of the whole battle continuing at La Maisonnette for a further three months, there would be no further advance in this area for the remainder of the battle.

The Attritional Battle (1) – the remainder of July 1916
North of the River
By the second week of July 1916, British failures in the northern part of the Somme battlefield, coupled with French and British successes in the south, had formed a dangerous salient in the allied line which was now dominated on three sides by a large quantity of German artillery and under constant threat from incessant counter-attacks. It became necessary to eliminate this salient and widen the angle of the frontline here. In order to accomplish this, the French army north of the river, coupled with a British north-easterly assault, would have to attack eastwards from the line between Hardecourt-aux-Bois in the north and Monacu Farm on the north bank of the Somme.

The church at Hardecourt aux Bois before the war.

The remains of Hardecourt following its capture.

To support this forthcoming Allied assault, the British Fourth Army began its next major assault on 14 July. Taking Trônes Wood, parts of Longueval, the Bazentins and the southern outskirts of Pozières, the British finally progressed beyond the German Second Line and eliminated some of the northerly threats to the advance. On the northern bank of the Somme river, *7e Corps d'armée* (under the command of *général de division* Georges de Bazelaire) began to move into the line south of *20e Corps d'armée*, as well as providing reinforcements to this battle weary formation.

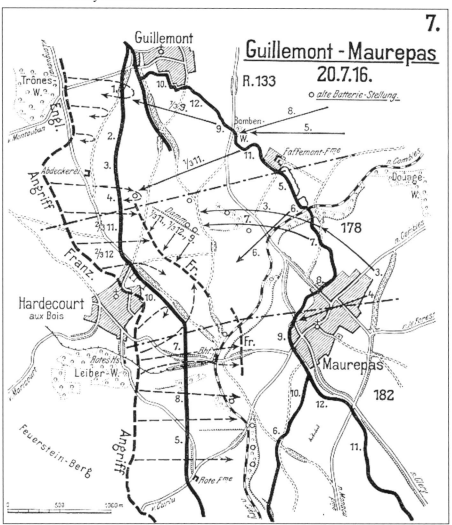

Guillemont – Maurepas, 20 July 1916 (from *Schlachten des Weltkrieges*).

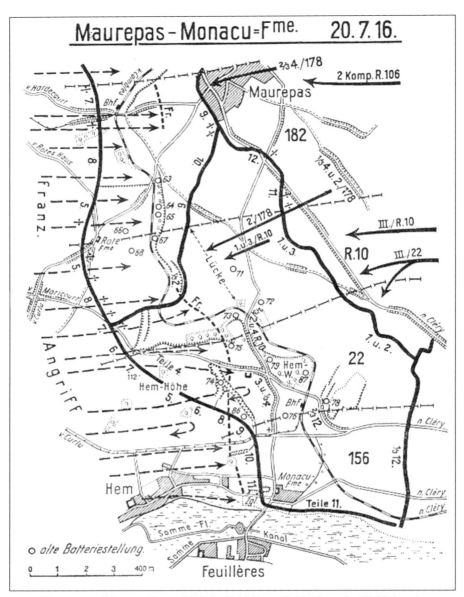

Maurepas – Monacu Farm, 20 July 1916 (from *Schlachten des Weltkrieges*).

On 20 July, thirteen German divisions serving in the Meuse sector and a further two from Flanders were transferred to the Somme to reinforce this front. Coinciding with this date, the French launched their part of this latest inter-Allied assault, attacking between Vermandovillers and Hardecourt-aux-Bois with mixed but very limited success. In many locations the French managed to enter and capture the German front lines but were invariably driven out by artillery fire and German counter-attacks, with the furthest advance being the single kilometre of ground gained over a three kilometre stretch of front line between the Bois de Hem and Maurepas Halte (between Maurepas and Hardecourt). Above the village of Hem, Hem Plateau was finally cleared. This was the most significant gain of the day; and a very harsh introduction to the Somme battle for the *153e* and *47e Divisions d'infanterie*, who had just moved into the front line a few days earlier in the northern portion of the French sector.

A further attack between Hem and Hardecourt on 23 July saw similar results and a slight advance in the front line; but another attack, launched on 30 July, was, perhaps, the most disastrous day for the French during the whole of the Battle of the Somme.

The fortified farm at Hem. It is in the grounds of this farm that the CWGC Hem Farm Military Cemetery is now located. A new farm was built to the east.

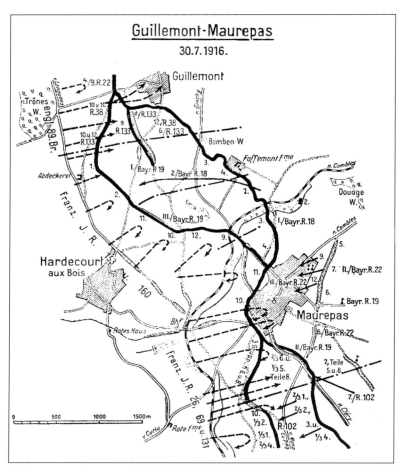

Guillemont – Maurepas, 30 July 1916 (from *Schlachten des Weltkrieges*).

Following a period of heavy shelling, the *41e*, *11e* and *39e Divisions d'infanterie* attacked at 04:45hrs but, in all but two places, failed to penetrate the German front line. Caught in a horrific machine gun crossfire and pounded by German artillery in No-Man's Land and their own front lines, all rearwards communication was lost as artillery severed the telephone cables. The shattered assault lines were left to fend for themselves as they were broken into isolated units operating with no command or orders and, all along the front, individuals and units were forced back to their original start line. Strong German counter-attacks forced all units that had broken through the front to retreat, surrender or die and just one single gain was attained and held (the southern section

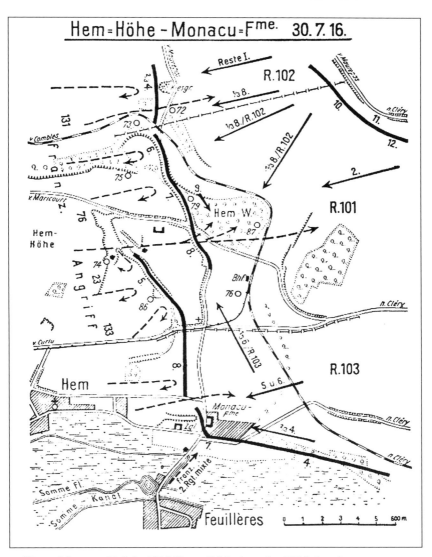

Hem - Monacu, 30 July 1916 (from *Schlachten des Weltkrieges*).

of the Bois de Hem, entered, captured and held by the *23e Régiment d'infanterie* at a cost of 519 casualties).

South of the River
Though the line remained largely static south of the river and, other than the actions around Biaches and La Maisonnette, whilst no further major

63

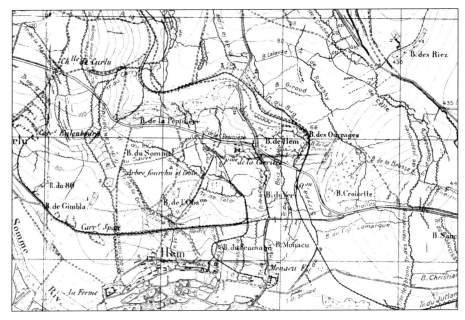

Hem Plateau Trench Map, September 1916.

actions could physically take place due to to the restrictions imposed by topography, the *1e Corps d'armée colonial* and *35e Corps d'armée* found themselves in action again as part of the general offensive of 20 July 1916. Located, at this time, near Barleux, the *16e Division d'infanterie coloniale*, just over a week after their sufferings at La Maisonnette, managed to enter the village on the 20th but, upon attempting further advances, found themselves caught in machine gun crossfire. Following a German counter-attack, they were back in their start positions by the end of the day and had suffered a further 2,000 casualties in the process.

Between Foucaucourt and Vermandovillers, *35e Corps d'armée*, reinforced by two extra divisions and artillery transferred from the north of the river, attacked towards Soyècourt and Vermandovillers. Managing to enter the northern parts of Soyècourt and capturing the whole of Bois Etoilé north west of Vermandovillers, the units here were also driven back by machine guns and artillery that preceded strong German counter-attacks by the end of the day. In this area the total gains amounted to just seventy metres of territory at a cost of over 4,000 casualties. There would be no further attacks in this area until September.

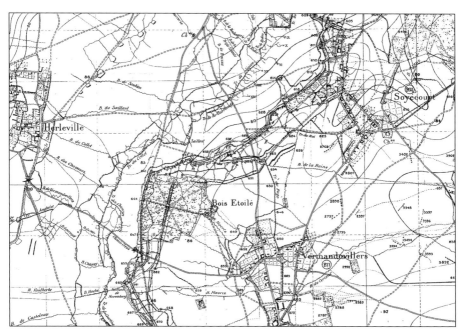

Vermandovillers – Soyécourt Trench Map, April 1916.

German trench in the centre of Soyécourt.

65

The Attritional Battle (2) – August 1916
North of the River

A month of steady advances for the French, August 1916 saw a set pattern of attack develop as the the line was straightened and gradually moved eastwards. Marked by a number of smaller scale actions, each advance was heralded by several days of bombardment before the infantry advanced a few hundred metres to the objective where, more often than not, vicious close quarter fighting took place before the newly won positions were consolidated and prepared for the inevitable German counter-attack. Each small scale objective was designed to be the jumping off point for the next objective and, following another bombardment, the process was repeated. The advance was costly and painfully slow, but an advance it was.

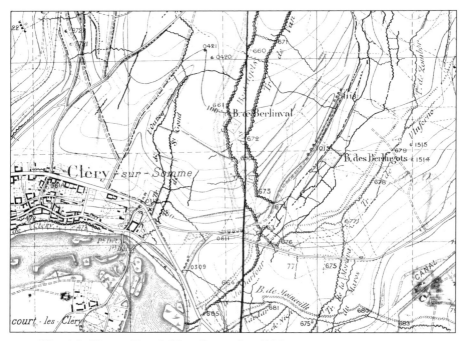

Montjoie Plateau Trench Map, September 1916.

During the first week of August the few remaining German positions on the Hem Plateau were taken, Monacu Farm was finally occupied, sections of the intermediate Somme River defensive line captured after a three day long battle dominated by extensive use of grenades and the

66

outskirts of the village of Clèry was reached in readiness for an imminent assault. On 12 August, following another sector wide offensive, almost the whole of the German Second Line from the western half of Maurepas down to the river fell to the French in what was described as 'a brilliant advance'; the only failures of the day taking place at the junction of the French and British forces near to where the British were attacking Guillemont. Further attacks on 18 and 24 August, in which Clèry was directly assaulted and partially captured, brought the remainder of the Second Line into French hands and placed Fayolle's *VIe Armée* in a position to advance on the intermediate line between the hamlet of Le Forest and Clèry, which would, in its turn, place the French in a position to attack the as yet incomplete German Third Line and then the open country beyond.

Clèry sur Somme as it appeared by the end of September 1916.

South of the River

With *général* Fayolle seemingly overstretched, having to control what had increasingly become two separate battles, operations south of the river were entrusted to *general* Micheler. The reserve corps, *2e Corps d'armée* (*général de division* Denis Auguste Duchêne), was moved into the front and inserted between *1e Corps d'armée coloniale* and *35e Corps d'armée*. With the extra artillery support and increase in troop numbers that came with this new corps, preparations began to continue the offensive in the south but this time directed in a south and south-easterly direction.

Other than in the extreme north around Biaches and, especially, La Maisonnette, where the fighting was almost constant throughout the month, the southern section of the Somme battlefield was relatively static throughout August. Notable only for artillery actions, patrols and raids, several small scale German counter attacks, intent upon altering the line and regaining advantageous positions, were successfully fought off. Though quiet at the front, the rear areas were extremely busy as the *Xe Armée* was made ready to go on the offensive.

The Attempted Breakthrough: September – November 1916
North of the River

By the end of August 1916, corps reliefs had placed the *1e*, *7e* and *33e Corps d'armée* (under the command of *générals de division* Marie Louis Adolphe Guillaumat, Georges de Bazelaire and Alphonse Pierre Nudant respectively) on *général* Fayolle's front in the north; with the *5e*, *6e* and *32e Corps d'armée* (*générals de division* Louis Etienne Auguste Hallouin, Marie-Jean-Auguste Paulinier and Henri Berthelot [soon to be replaced by *général de division* Marie-Eugène Debeney]) in reserve, ready to exploit any successes. As it had become apparent by now that it was a logistical nightmare to attempt to get all of the Somme armies to attack simultaneously, it would now be up to the *VIe Armée* to break the German centre and enable a possibly significant advance along the River Somme.

Designed as a two stage, assault first against the Le Forest line and then aginst the Third Line between Rancourt and the river, the overall intention, in conjunction with British attacks at Thiepval, the Ancre valley, positions between Martinpuich and Guillemont and the Third Line between Le Sars and Morval, was to move the stagnating British Army line forward. The following day, Micheler's *Xe Armée* would launch its southern attack between Barleux and Chilly, extending the whole offensive to the south.

Launched, after another delay due to the weather, on 3 September 1916, the French attackers consisted (from the river northwards) of the *70e, 77e, 1e* and *2e Divisions d'infanterie*. Distributed amongst these were the *45e, 46e, 47e* and *66e Divisions d'infanterie*, each containing battalions of colonial troops or *chasseurs á pied*, along with two independent assault brigades, the *4e Brigade de chasseurs á pied* and the *6e Brigade de chasseurs alpins*. Though only partially successful in the northern extremeties, this attack was a spectacular success immediately north of the river. Backed by an extremely effective supporting barrage, the French smashed through position after position and the guns managed to restrict the activity of German batteries, rendering any attempted counter bombardment relatively ineffective. Clèry fell to the *66e Division*

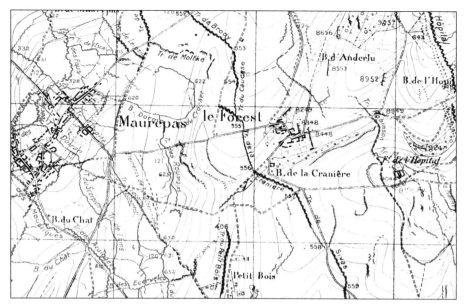

Maurepas – le Forest Trench Map, September 1916.

Domestic detritus – all that was left of le Forest after the tide of war had passed.

d'infanterie, Le Forest was taken in a classic enveloping move by the *2e* and *46e Divisions d'infanterie* and some of the advanced German gun lines beyond, such as those at the Ferme de l'Hôpital (taken by the *2e* and *26e Divisions d'infanterie*) were taken and they even managed to capture a tethered observation balloon.

In support of the *Xe Armée* attack south of the river on 4th September, the *VIe Armée* advance was continued across the plateau south of Combles until it was within assaulting distance of the German Third Line. Clèry was consolidated and the line pushed beyond the village (the front would remain here until the end of the battle), whilst the isolated German held hamlet of Omiécourt-lès-Cléry on the river loop in the marshes south of the river was captured. The *6e* and *28e Brigades de chasseurs alpines* launched an attack on the cluster of woods before the German Third Line (Bois Reinette, Bois Marrières and Bois Madame), managing to secure all objectives within three hours at the cost of some 670 casualties. The German defenders in the area, fearing a breakthrough, retired to the Third Line, but, against stiffer opposition here, the French attack faltered and was halted in order for the guns to be brought further forward and preparations made for the next stage.

The outpost hamlet of Omiécourt-les-Cléry soon after its capture in September 1916.

Keen to press the advantage before the Germans managed to strengthen their defences, Foch and Fayolle were frustrated in their plans by events that were to force a delay to the continuing advance. The weather began to create resupply problems to the new positions at the front and most of the reserves had been used up in the advance as it fanned out across the plateau. They had also advanced beyond the British and were forced to construct a defensive perimeter on the northern flank, thus using even more reserves and forcing new divisions to be deployed. It would eventually be 12 September before the advance could be continued.

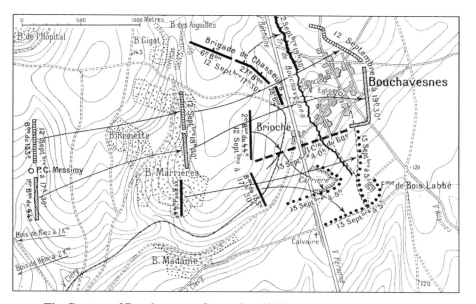

The Capture of Bouchavesnes, September 1916.

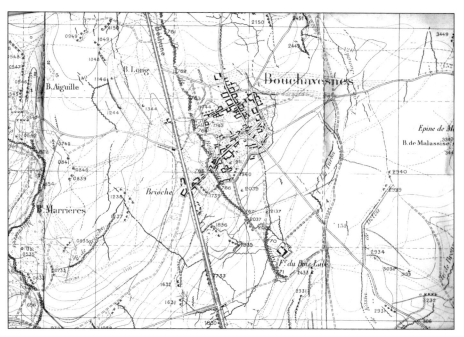

Bouchavesnes Trench Map, September 1916.

71

The largest French attack to date for the French north of the Somme took place on 12 September 1916. Three *Corps d'armée,* with five divisions in the initial assault, attacked the German line between the hamlet of Frègicourt (east of Combles) and the river. Objectives within this area included the formidable fortified villages of Rancourt, Sailly-Saillisel and Bouchavesnes; with the ultimate objectives being the Tortille river valley, Mont St Quentin and, optimistically, even turning the defences at Péronne.

Throughout the next few days, the French managed to exploit early successes, capturing six kilometres of German Third Line and pushing forwards three kilometres in the central area of the attack. The Bois de Berlingots was captured (then lost, then captured again!) north of Cléry on the first day, though no further advance was possible, the eastern edge becoming the established frontline, as was the village of Bouchavesnes to the north. Above and beyond here, however, artillery from the German batteries on Mont St Quentin forced the advance to stall. Unobserved movement was difficult and, coupled with machine gun fire from numerous positions located in the huge Bois St Pierre Vaast, further advance became almost suicidal. The strong point at the Ferme du Bois l'Abbé east of Bouchavesnes was captured but, like the line to the south, this would become a dangerously exposed French front line position for the remainder of the battle.

The church at Bouchavesnes, September 1916.

A French *poste de secours* set up in the old quarry near Bouchavesnes.

In the northern sector of the attack, the French succeeded in capturing Le Priez Ferme after two days of fighting and managed to advance towards Rancourt cemetery before being stopped by artillery and machine gun fire; but failed completely before Frègicourt and Sailly-Saillisel.

Though progress was practically static by 15 September, the French continued with aggressive actions in the northern sector in support of the British operations to their west. Using fatigued troops and with a minimal artillery preparation, the only real successes of the day were in keeping the German reserves in the area occupied.

Following these actions, the *VIe Armée* sector was heavily reinforced with the *5e, 6e* and *32e Corps d'armée* moving into the line between the *1e* and *33e Corps d'armée* in order to alleviate the problems caused by the widening French front, which was now twelve kilometres longer than it had been on 12 September, and in preparation for the next large scale attack. At the same time as the British Fourth Army attack (12.25pm) on 25 September 1916, the *VIe Armée* launched their assault on the northern fringe of the Somme battlefield. Progress was good in the vicinity of Combles; Rancourt fell to the *42e Division d'infanterie* within the first hour and an advance towards Frègicourt enabled the hamlet to be captured during the early hours of the following day. French troops

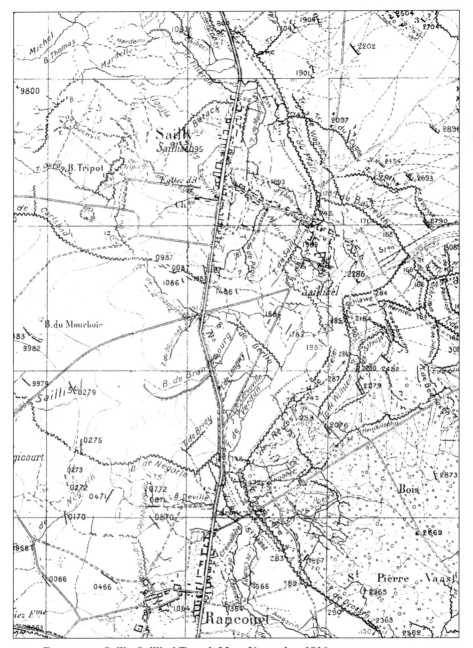

Rancourt – Sailly-Saillisel Trench Map, November 1916.

74

The Bapaume road at Rancourt before the war.

penetrated the north western section of Bois St Pierre Vaast. Combles was captured jointly by the French and British on 26 September and an advance to assault distance on Sailly-Saillisel made. Further south, however, an advance beyond Bouchavesnes again proved impossible and, beyond Rancourt, the attack faltered against the massed machine guns of Bois St Pierre Vaast.

A typical scene towards the end of the battle. The aftermath of another assault near Bois St Pierre Vaast.

75

Sailly-Saillisel – the scene of some of the most vicious house to house fighting of the war – at the end of the Battle of the Somme.

Throughout October and into November there was a stalemate. Large scale offensive operations recommenced on 6 October but in the mud caused by an almost continuous downpour of rain movement was difficult even without the German defenders. Launched in the afternoon of 6 October, in conjunction with a diversionary assault on Bois St Pierre Vaast, the *40e Division d'infanterie* managed to reach the outskirts of Sailly-Saillisel but were forced to halt and dig in before the village was finally entered on the night of 15/16 October. Continuous fighting – possibly some of the worst fighting in which the French Army was

Sailly-Saillisel before the war. Traffic was obviously not then a problem.

involved during the whole Battle of the Somme - for the village raged for the remainder of the month, with two further attacks, on the 11 and 14 November 1916 finally pushed the Germans out.

With the front line located just to Sailly-Saillisel's northern and eastern boundaries, before running southwards along the western fringe of Bois St Pierre Vaast, east of Bouchavesnes, along the eastern fringe of Bois de Berlingots, and to the east of Cléry-sur-Somme to the river, the line in this area stabilised for the remainder of the battle. Here it continued to be the stage for many small scale unit actions, all without any conclusive results.

Very relieved looking infantrymen returning to billets following front line service at the end of the Battle of the Somme.

South of the River

Restricted in the northern section south of the river by the curvature of the River Somme, *géneral* Micheler's *Xe Armée* was tasked with the extension of the offensive to the south. Extending the southern limit of the offensive as far as Maucourt, the attack drove in a southerly and south easterly direction, capturing the German defences between Barleux and Chilly, crossing the Santerre plateau and hinging in an eastwards direction towards the northerly flowing River Somme. It was also hoped that it would be possible to exploit a German collapse and take the Somme crossings south of Péronne and pursue the offensive on the eastern bank. It was planned to perform a sustained four phase assault behind the usual curtain of artillery fire but, due to continued fierce fighting at Verdun still being a drain on resources and the priority being given to the *VIe Armée* in the north, *Xe Armée* was more reliant on its own resources, which resulted in the opening bombardment being far less overwhelming than was hoped. Just two days before the attack it was reported that there were still huge parts of the German defences that remained practically untouched. It was apparent that in this sector the infantry would have to be less reliant on artillery.

The German defences consisted of two lines that would have to be assaulted. In the north, between Barleux and Soyécourt, though it had already seen heavy fighting since July, the defences had not been destroyed. This line turned southwards to the west of Soyécourt into the pre-July front which, as far down as Chilly, had been worked upon and fortified since September 1914. All along the line were the strongly fortified villages of Barleux, Berny-en-Santerre, Deniécourt, Soyécourt, Vermandovillers and Chilly, reinforced to the rear by similarly fortified locations such as Villers-Carbonnel, Mazancourt, Ablaincourt, Pressoir and the all important railhead of Chaulnes (which was in turn protected to the west and north by a complicated group of heavily defended and interconnected woodland). An advance in this sector – even with adequate artillery support – was never going to be an easy task.

At 2pm on 4 September 1916, following on from the offensive launched north of the river, the *Xe Armée* launched its attack after a six day bombardment. Ten French divisions moved forward against five strongly entrenched German divisions. In the extreme south, the *20e Division d'infanterie* stormed the village of Chilly and advanced beyond it, capturing the trio of woods to the north east of the village. Advancing down the railway line towards the Chaulnes railhead, the attack was halted beyond Bois Browning, about a kilometre short of the final objective, preventing a further advance on Chaulnes. Opposite Lihons and north of Chaulnes, the heavily defended woods proved an insurmountable obstacle for the attacking *10e Corps d'armée,* but a foothold in the western edges was gained. Further north, the *10e Corps d'armée* attack was stopped dead in its tracks by the machine guns in the heavily fortified Bois Blockhaus opposite Lihu Ferme.

North of Lihu, opposite Vermandovillers, the *132e Division d'infanterie* attacked through Bois Etoilé and approached the village, where the German defences proved to be too strong. Despite fighting their way into the village, German pressure forced the French back to the old German trenches in Bois Etoilé .With the line now held on the eastern fringe of the wood, the next five days saw several other fruitless attempts to move forward and occupy Vermandovillers.

At the 'hinge' of the line that joined the pre-July front line with that of the pre-September southern flank of the Somme offensive, the ruins of Soyécourt were seized by the *43e Division d'infanterie* after being assaulted from both the north and the west with the aid of an extremely effective artillery barrage. Further along the line, the northern outskirts

The rear of Lihu Farm as it was during the spring of 1915.

of the villages of Deniécourt and Berny-en-Santerre were reached but could not be taken, thereby exposing the attacking troops at Soyécourt to machine gun fire from the flanks and preventing further progress there as well; and at Barleux, the *77e Division d'infanterie*, after advancing under extremely heavy fire through the German front line, became caught on the uncut German wire in front of the village. With German defenders emerging from undamaged shelters *behind* the attackers, the forward troops were cut off and systematically destroyed. Reserves sent forward to assist were scythed down in No Man's Land in front of the reoccupied German forward positions and the attack ended in abject failure.

French infantry preparing for action at Vermandovillers, 4 September 1916.

On 5 September, a large scale German counter-attack along this southern front was successfully repulsed and the French advance continued to stagger stutteringly forwards; half of the village of Berny-en-Santerre fell to the French during the afternoon and slight advances were made at Vermandovillers, with the *1e Bataillon de chasseurs à pied* successfully occupying the ground in front of the village cemetery by the 6th. Movement elsewhere along the line was minimal as the new front was consolidated, straightened and strengthened. In the light of several German counter-attacks, and with the threat of more to come, Micheler called off the general offensive on 7 September and decided instead to concentrate on specific targets from then on. At this point, the French had taken some 6,650 prisoners and captured thirty six artillery pieces (including twenty eight heavies) but, due to insufficient artillery preparation along most of the line, had suffered heavy losses and failed to gain many of the objectives, rendering the offensive, in the words of French post-war historians, as a 'half failure'.

Following a week long bombardment on the German line between Vermandovillers and Berny-en-Santerre, the attack was resumed in the northern part of this sector. Vermandovillers finally fell to the *120e Division d'infanterie* during the evening of 17 September and the remainder of Berny-en-Santerre was captured by the *4e Division d'infanterie* at about the same time. Deniécourt was seized during the early hours of the following day and, with this northern flank now open, a steady, but gradual, advance could be made across the open land crossing the Ablaincourt Ridge.

The next major target for Micheler was the first day objective town of Chaulnes and its railhead where the offensive had stuttered and then been halted at the opening of the offensive. With the French line closing in to the north of the town, the next assault took place on 10 October. Attacked by the *51e Division d'infanterie*, progress was made in the west,

Vermandovillers church and churchyard – the scene of some of the heroic actions of the *166e* and *366e Régiments d'infanterie* during the first week of September 1916.

The remains of Génermont Sucrerie, October 1916.

with a foothold gained in the western part of the town and a slight advance made towards the railhead in the south. In the north, however, the attackers came upon massed machine guns and defences in the group of numbered woods making up the Bois de Chaulnes and were halted. A German counter-attack on the 11th drove the French completely out of Chaulnes and began a long protracted battle within the woods to the north, during which a complete battalion of French infantry (from the *25e Régiment d'infanterie*) was annihilated within a few hours. Hand-to-hand (and tree-to-tree!) fighting continued in this woodland for much of the remainder of the battle.

A shell bursting on the remains of the hamlet of Génermont, October 1916.

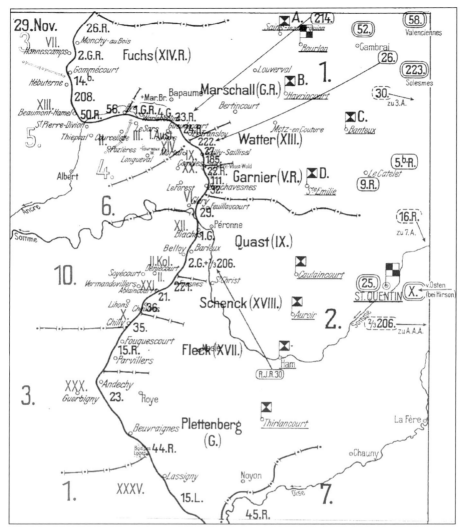

The Somme Front, 29 November 1916 (from *Der Weltkrieg 1914 bis 1918*).

On 14 October, the *120e Division d'infanterie* managed to break off Ablaincourt Ridge and push on towards the village of Ablaincourt with the *13e Division d'infanterie* to their left moving towards Fresnes, capturing the sugar factory and hamlet of Genermont in the process. A week later, on 21 October, a surprise attack north of Chaulnes was nearly successful in clearing the Germans out of Bois de Chaulnes. However, a strong German counter attack on the 22nd restored the positions to their

21 October location. This action was typical of how the offensive was now to progress within this sector into November. The final attack along any length of this front took place on 7 November. During this action the French once again failed to break through Bois de Chaulnes but, to the north east, the village of Ablaincourt and its associated hamlet of Pressoire fell to the *62e Division d'infanterie*, thereby ending the offensive in this specific area. A massive German counter attack on Ablaincourt on 25 November 1916 was successfully defended by this same division, who did not concede even a metre of territory.

The Final Act – Chaulnes

Located within a narrow salient by November 1916, Chaulnes had proven a constant thorn in Micheler's side since the opening day of his September offensive. Rather than launch a direct assault to the west and north of the town, as had been the case in the previous four failed attempts to take the town, it was proposed that the next attack – scheduled for 5 December 1916 – should concentrate all efforts on the north. A double brigade sized assault would be carried out by the *13e* and *4e Divisions d'infanterie* from the centre of Bois de Chaulnes as far as Génermont, with diversionary fire being provided by the *62e Division d'infanterie*. Intended to take the villages of Hyencourt and Gomiécourt, taking parts of the German Second Line north of Chaulnes, it was hoped to weaken

Chaulnes after the German withdrawal of 1917.

CHAULNES. - La Rue de Lihons - Lihons Street

the northern defences and enable a southerly advance to encircle and therefore capture the town, entering at its north-eastern corner.

On 5 December, following a short preliminary bombardment, the attack was launched. All along the attacking front the French failed to penetrate the German line as they floundered in the freezing mud before the German wire. Bois 4 within Bois de Chaulnes was finally captured, concluding a two month struggle for this section of wood; but it proved impossible to progress beyond. To the east and up to Bois Kratz no further gains were made within the woods. The attack was cancelled by evening and plans begun for a further assault.

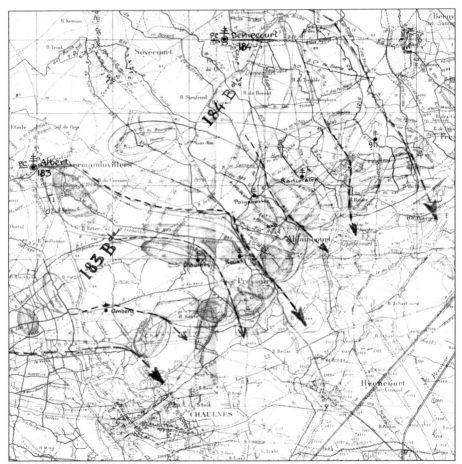

Chaulnes Trench Map, December 1916, with annotations depicting the attack of 5 December.

Similar to the 5 December attack, the next assault on Chaulnes was to come from the north. Scheduled for 13 December, the preparatory bombardment began on the night of 7/8 December but, due to bad weather, the attack was postponed until 18 December and then rescheduled to the 20th to enable further softening up of the German defences.

On 12 December 1916, however, *général* Robert Georges Nivelle replaced *général* Foch as the commander of the *groupe d'armées Nord* and did not see the value of capturing Chaulnes given the cost in resources and human lives that it had already claimed. On 17 December 1916, therefore, he cancelled all large scale offensive operations around Chaulnes and along the French Somme line as a whole. The 171 days of the French army's part in the Battle of the Somme were now over.

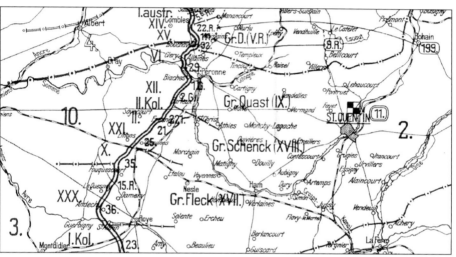

The Somme Front, 16 December 1916 (from *Der Weltkrieg 1914 bis 1918*).

The Result

In almost five and a half months of the Somme offensive the Allies had managed to push the front eastwards by some ten to twelve kilometres at best. The breakthrough, which had been ultimately hoped for by Joffre, enabling the use of cavalry beyond the trenches and a return to a war of movement, had proven to be an impossible dream and neither of the principal towns in the area, Bapaume and Péronne (just thirteen and ten kilometres behind the 1 July front lines respectively), had been captured. In the French sector, the key observation and artillery positions of Mont St Quentin and La Maisonnette were still in German hands, as was the

Chaulnes railhead and all of the Somme river crossings south of Péronne.

By the second week of July, however, the Somme was certainly living up to its primary role - that of a battle of attrition – and it was eventually successful in diverting German reserves and attention away from Verdun, thereby successfully relieving the crisis that had enveloped the French Army there. Another positive factor resulting from this battle was that it was realised that inter-army cooperation could win battles, especially when overall command was given to one person. The French who, up to the launch of the Battle of the Somme, had been more than a little suspicious about the British commitment to the war, also realised that in fact the British were a serious ally who could be trusted to operate alongside them in joint operations. Though not a victory as such, the battle was certainly a strategic success for the Allies.

In the course of the offensive, the French Army on the Somme captured somewhere in the region of 41,605 German prisoners (including over 800 officers), seventy one field guns, 101 heavy guns, 104 mortars and 535 machine guns. Sources – almost needless to say – disagree about casualties; an authorative source states that the French suffered 202,567 casualties throughout the battle of whom 66,688 were recorded as killed or missing. To illustrate the rate of attrition on the Somme, the daily casualty rate for the French on the Somme was just under 200 more than the daily casualty rate at Verdun!

French graves in the chateau park of Sailly-Saillisel after the battle – a common scene of utter desolation and human misery all over the Somme battlefield.

Chapter Four

Tours of the French Sector

Introduction and Advice to Tourers

As was the case for the French during the Battle of the Somme, the following tours have been split into three distinct sections: north of the river, south of the river and the southern 'extension' battle. The first two tours (north of the river and south of the river) are also split chronologically and geographically, the first part of each covering (mainly) the 1 July actions, leading onto the second part (and, in the case for the north of the river, a third part), which covers the actions following this first day of battle. The second part of each tour begins where the first part ends, enabling the visitor to either cover just the section of their choice, or cover the entire tour as a whole. The third tour is complete in one part.

Approximate distances covered in each tour are as follows:

Tour 1: 71 kilometres (in three parts – 14.5, 19.5 and 37 kilometres)
Tour 2: 48 kilometres (in two parts – 16 and 32 kilometres)
Tour 3: 29 kilometres

Covering practically the whole of the French area of combat during the 1916 Battle of the Somme (either physically or within view), the tours have been designed to be practicable by mini-bus, car, motorbike and bicycle (and, of course, foot for the more hardy traveller!). Larger vehicles may have problems in a few locations as several of the roads are quite narrow. These, however, are generally rather open with passing places; there are a couple of sharp turns and one low bridge to negotiate, thus, for anyone planning to use a larger bus, a pre-tour reconnaisance is strongly recommended.

Within the tours, locations have been referred to using their French war time names. A select gazetteer of some of these locations, where they differ to the British war time names (even if they are direct translations), can be found immediately after the tour section in the order in which they appear within the tours.

GPS References. Note that at the end of each tour section there is a list of GPS references for each of the numbered stop points within that tour.

Maps

Recommended mapping for the area (some of the routes are quite complex) are the topographical 1:25,000 scale IGN Blue Series or 'Top 25' *cartes de randonée*. To completely cover the French sector of the 1916 battle, the following maps from this series would be needed: 2408 E (Bray-sur-Somme), 2508 O (Péronne), 2409 E (Roye) and 2509 O Nesle. The 1:100,000 scale IGN 'Top 100' Yellow Series tourism road map number 103 (Amiens/Arras) also covers the area in lesser detail. For historical interest, the IGN have also produced a centennial edition map of the 1916 Somme battle area in 1: 75,000 scale entitled '*Grande Guerre: Bataille de la Somme 1916*' which, though not error-free, details divisional locations for the 1st July, the battle lines and certain movements along with (some) cemeteries, memorials and visitable vestiges of the battle, etc. (This is part of a special series of maps produced by the IGN, others being maps for the Battle of Verdun 1916, the Chemin des Dames 1917 and, generically, the Western Front 1914-18.)

British trench maps for the area are readily viewable from a variety of online sources. The Great War Digital offering of the 'Linesman' package is highly recommended which, with the aid of a compatable portable GPS device, enables the visited area to be viewed using period trench maps. Recently, the company has released a preloaded selection of trench maps on a tablet that makes a more user-friendly option available for the less computer literate. Bearing in mind, however, that with all available maps for this package currently being British, this is less useful for the areas south of the river, where coverage is limited just to the pre-1 July area down to the Amiens – St Quentin road and the final battle lines south of Péronne. Though the areas fought over in between these dates are still covered by maps of various dates within this package (and on online sources), the most useful ones post date the battle. French trench maps are ideally needed for these areas, but these are a harder to source (though several extracts are to be found in this book).

Accommodation

Plentiful hotel accommodation can be found in the area of the battlefields with Péronne, Bapaume and Albert – in that order – being the most suitably located main towns for visits to the French Somme battlefield (with Amiens being reserved as a decent alternative should accommodation prove scarce during peak periods). A number of well known hotel chains operate in these areas. Bed and breakfast accommodation is also plentiful and can be found in many of the villages of the British sectors of the battlefield. Highly recommended is Dave and Anita Platt's 'Beaumont Hamel View', located at 15 Rue Delattre,

Auchonvillers (http://www.beaumonthamelview.com). Though similar accommodation is scarcer in the southern French sector, a small number do exist, as do a few 'Gîtes de France' self-catering cottages, which can be located and booked from their English language website: https://en.gites-de-france.com. The northern French sector is better serviced, being located within easy driving/riding distance from many of the 'British' sites (though the self catering cottages of 'Chavasse Farm' (http://www.chavasseferme.com) and the self catering gîte of 'Fairbanks' (http://lesalouettes.net/fairbanks-gite) along with the bed and breakfast accommodation of 'Les Alouettes' (http://lesalouettes.net/bed-breakfast) – all at Hardecourt-aux-Bois- are within the northern French, rather than the British, sector).

For camping, the ideally located, three star, Camping du Port de Plaisance at Péronne (http://www.camping-plaisance.com), which is within easy strolling distance from the town centre or Biaches and centrally placed for visits to both the northern and southern French battlefield, has a small shop, bar, take-away and swimming pool and is also near to a petrol station and supermarket. This camp site also happens to be built on the site of the *ouvrage du faubourg de Paris,* which was a small defensive fort that played a role in the siege of Péronne in 1870-71 and served as (German) soldiers accommodation during 1914-1917. Though nothing is visible of this *ouvrage* today, watch out when hammering in those tent-pegs!

A number of other, smaller, camp sites also exist along the Somme River (often geared to fishing), including one at the infamous Grenouillére position near Frise.

Refreshments

Apart from the ubiquitous *boulangeries* and local village cafés and bars, refreshment stops are a rare commodity in the French sector. It is, therefore, advisable to stock up with any necessary supplies from the more considerable towns in the area. Péronne, Albert, Bapaume and Chaulnes – one of which will always be within eleven or twelve kilometres from your location on these tours – are all well served by supermarkets, cafés, bars and restaurants, with the larger supermarkets in these towns containing all of these, plus petrol stations, in one location. All of the facilities (other than the petrol station) at the motorway service station at Asseviliers can also be accessed on foot from the car park located at the end of the side road that will be used to study the *légion étrangère* attack on Belloy-en-Santerre. This is often open when the others are closed, so can be quite a handy stop. Finally, the *Historial de la Grande Guerre* at Péronne has a café and, should the need arise,

McDonald's restaurants can be found at Albert, Péronne, Roye, Montdidier and Amiens (which has four!)

Museums

The French sector is nowhere near as well served with museums as the British. The French 1916 Somme battlefield has two main museums, the *Musée Somme 1916* at Albert and the *Historial de la Grande Guerre* at Péronne.

Located within shooting distance of the furthest French advance during the 1916 battle, the *Historial de la Grande Guerre* (http://www.historial.org) is, other than the small display at Rancourt, the only museum actually located within (or, to be more accurate, beyond) the French area of operations of 1916.

Attracting over 80,000 visitors per year, the tri-lingual displays and exhibitions aim to illustrate the experiences of the major combattants and the impact of the Great War in general on the 20th century as well as the experiences of those involved in the Battles of the Somme, including the civilian population. Housing several temporary exhibitions at any one time alongside the more permanent features, film shows and display cases, art and technology also features prominently.

Display cases and information panels explain the course of the war from its origins to the post-war reconstructions and a rather original method of display educates the visitor on the uniforms and equipment of the protaganists.

Built within the remains of the heavily repaired walls of the old 13th century Château de Péronne (look for the memorial plaque above the entrance to the *120e* and *320e Régiments d'infanterie* and the *16e Régiment d'infanterie territoriale* – who had their depot here in August 1914), there is a Documentation Centre within the museum; accessible by appointment only, this aims to provide an international approach to the study of the military, political and cultural history of the Great War and holds an archive of photographs, postcards, leaflets and other documents on the Great War along with a library of over 4,000 books and periodicals.

A decent café with terrace that can cater for groups and a variably stocked shop selling books in numerous languages, DVDs, maps, posters and other souvenirs can also be found at the museum (though the Thiepval Visitor Centre, run by the Historial, has a far better and more extensive selection)

Within the French rear area can be found another museum. Though it is not a museum of the battle as such, it is an extremely interesting diversion anyway. Located at Froissy, south of and on the opposite river

The memorial to the local regiments of Péronne.

bank from Bray-sur-Somme, the *P'tit Train de la Haute Somme* houses a narrow-gauge railway museum displaying several engines of Great War vintage. The highlight of a visit here, however, is a ride on a fourteen kilometre stretch of narrow-gauge railway line that was originally built in 1916 to move ammunition and supplies to the artillery and forward areas south of the River Somme (post-war it was used by the sucrerie at Dompierre). Travelling up onto the Santerre plateau as far as Dompierre, it is a very interesting ride with some beautiful views.

A Decauville military railway transporting ammunition (in this case, ammunition for the *Mortier de 370 mm Modèle 1887* railway gun) near Proyart. This was part of the same network that can be seen (and ridden) today at Froissy.

Toilet Facilities

Toilets can be located at most of the places mentioned in the refreshments section (though it is usually regarded as courteous to actually buy something first if using the facilities in a local bar/café). Additional to these, there are also facilities to be found in the visitor centre at the *Nécropole Nationale* at Rancourt.

Clothing and Footwear

None of the ground covered in the tours is particularly difficult, but several locations will require walking over rough ground in order to appreciate the location fully. The Somme is not particularly extreme for weather conditions, but common sense (and, perhaps, a look at the local weather forecast) should dictate clothing and footwear. One point to bear in mind, however, is that in a number of locations, such as on the Flaucourt Plateau, the tours visit areas that are extremely open, exposed and with not much shelter. For this reason, it may be advisable to pack some sort of sun protection, carry a bottle of water and cover up on hot summer days. Likewise, keep water-proof and wind-proof clothing handy for days that are less clement (sage advice from someone who was once caught in a howling thunder storm in the middle of a field on the Flaucourt Plateau wearing a T-shirt, shorts and sandals!). In all cases, especially if you anticipate doing some walking, it is a good idea to have some stout boots handy. Even if they are not needed at the outset of a tour, the changeable weather and topography of the Somme could make them necessary by the end. A further tip would be to keep a plastic bag in which to put your boots before getting back into a vehicle, saving you from carting considerable quantities of Somme mud around with you and spreading it around your vehicle – it is very tenacious!

Tour 1: North of the Somme
Part 1 – 1 July specific

Beginning the tour at the village of **Suzanne (1)**, on the north bank of the River Somme, we are starting in what was, perhaps, one of the most hectic rear villages in the run up to the Battle of the Somme north of the river. The location of the *160e Régiment d'infanterie* in Corps Reserve on 1 July 1916, it was also an artillery hub, with some seventy two French artillery batteries of varying calibres (mainly between 75mm and 105 mm, with one 270 mm battery located on the northern outskirt of the village) within two kilometers to the north and east.

*From the centre of Suzanne, take the Vaux road (running parallel with the river) towards Éclusier-Vaux and Vaux itself. At the Éclusier roundabout, reached after two kilometres and located at the south-east corner of the Bois du Royal Dragons (Bois Fauvel) continue left towards Vaux. [It is possible here to make a short detour across the river by turning right. Upon reaching the far bank of the river, an immediate right turn will take you, after 500 metres, to the **communal cemetery (2)** containing over a hundred French war graves from 1914-1918 and twenty three British war graves from early 1917].*

*After turning left at the roundabout (or travelling straight on if returning from the Éclusier detour), we travel past the Bois du Royal Dragons and follow the road into **Vaux**, taking the right hand fork in the road some 200 metres beyond the village cemetery.*

On the hill top to the left is located **Bois de Vaux**. Still containing the remains of trenches and shell holes, etc. from the 1916 to 1918 period, this wood was occupied by the *69e Régiment d'infanterie* (held in Divisional Reserve on 1 July 1916) and was also the location of the command post of the *11e Division d'Infanterie*.

*Continue on this road, following the course of the river and around the loop of the River Somme. After just over two kilometres, the tiny hamlet (in reality an extended farm) of **Fargny (3)** is reached. On the right, on the river bank, can be seen the site of Fargny Mill (**Moulin de Fargny**).*

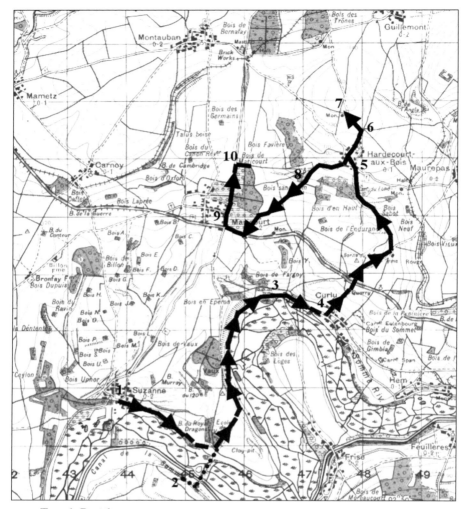

Tour 1, Part 1.

The scene of a small skirmish between French infantry controlling a Somme crossing point and German cavalry in December 1870, this was a frontline position in July 1916. For the past year a bizarre state of 'live and let live' had existed and it was noted by various diarists that the 'fishing was good' here! Soldiers from both sides took the opportunity to bathe in the waters of the Somme, wash clothes and embark on fishing expeditions, often in full view of each other. This would all change, however, in the run up to the Battle of the Somme, when the Moulin de

The *Moulin de Fargny*, with the *Chapeau de Gendarme* in the background.

The Somme at Fargny today. The *Chapeau de Gendarme* is the tree covered area to the left of the photograph.

French cavalrymen at rest in front of the *Chapeau de Gendarme*. The French front line of 1 July was located just ahead of the group of men standing in the middle distance, with the German front being just forward of the horizon.

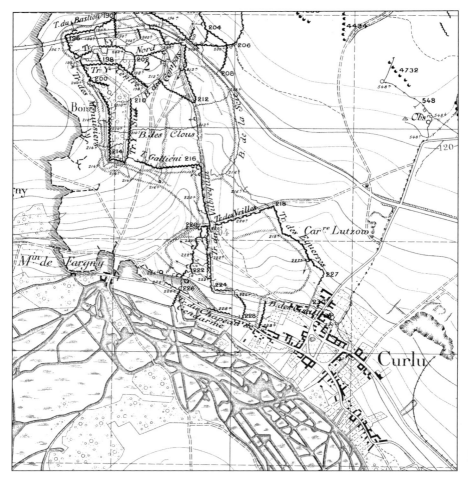

Fargny – Curlu Trench Map, June 1916.

Fargny would become the advanced jumping off point for the *37e Régiment d'infanterie* in their assault on the village of Curlu.

Continue on the river road towards **Curlu (4)***.*

We are now traversing the route taken by the southernmost attacking troops of the 3rd Battalion of the *37e Régiment d'infanterie* at 7.30am on 1 July 1916. Protected from the north by the steep banking to the left (part of a feature known, due to its shape, as the *Chapeau de Gendarme*), this area was relatively lightly defended. The German front line was located approximately half way along this banking and was defended by

96

a single machine gun on the bank itself (covering the road on which we are now travelling) and another at the top of the bank, which was more concerned with engaging the *37e Régiment d'infanterie* attacking to the north of this position. The road itself was heavily barricaded and the majority of attackers in this area fought their way down the *Tranchée du Chapeau de Gendarme,* which ran a couple of metres or so north of and parallel with the road directly into the village of Curlu. By 8am, the *3ᵉ Bataillon* had entered the village and, encountering stiff resistance, had begun to clear the remains of buildings using grenades and bayonets, pushing on as far as the church, where they came under heavy machine gun fire.

To the north of the village, the *2ᵉ Bataillon* of the *37e Régiment d'infanterie,* who attacked from the vicinity of the Bois de Fargny and advanced over the plain to the north of the *Chapeau de Gendarme,* were also stopped mid morning by machine guns in Curlu and the old phosphate quarries to the north. In the early afternoon, a counter-attack was successfully repulsed and many casualties inflicted on the German attackers; at 6pm, following a violent bombardment, the attack was renewed and the village (except for a few buildings on the eastern outskirts) was captured by 7pm. All objectives taken, the front line now

The road from Fargny to Curlu. It was down this road that elements of the *37e Régiment d'infanterie* advanced on 1 July.

extended from the south eastern edge of Curlu village, up through the *carrière de Eulenbourg* (marking the demarcation line between the *3ᵉ Bataillon* to the south and the *2ᵉ Bataillon* to the north) and across to the *carrière Lutzow* near the main road to Péronne. The *37e Régiment d'infanterie* suffered some 200 casualties in the capture of Curlu.

Take the first road to the left upon entering Curlu and drive northwards.

The 1 July battlefield of the *37e* and *79e Régiments d'infanterie* (advancing towards the camera).

Looking to the left as we travel up this road, you will see the fields across which the *2ᵉ Bataillon* of the *37e Régiment d'infanterie* attacked on 1 July 1916. Just after the slight left swing in the road, there are the remains of an old phosphate quarry on the left. This is the *carrière Lutzow*, site of one of the machine gun positions that caused so much trouble and a successfully carried objective for the *37e Régiment d'infanterie* on the opening day of the battle. It became a front line position at the end of the first day.

Carrière Lutzow – a German strongpoint and the southern limit of the first day advance of the *79e Régiment d'infanterie*.

Cross the D938. Approximately 900 metres from the D938, take the left fork at the Y junction just beyond Ferme Rouge on the right (this was a fortified position that was finally captured on 20 July 1916) to the village of **Hardecourt-aux-Bois (5)**.

Not an objective for 1 July 1916, Hardecourt-aux-Bois became a front line village following this date. Located just behind the German front line during the French consolidation period from the evening of 1 July, it was a target in the Anglo-French attacks of 8 July (originally intended for the 7th, but delayed due to a German attack on Bois Favière) when the *39e Division d'infanterie* launched an assault on the western slopes of Hardecourt Ridge and on the village. At dawn on 8 July, under the cover of a heavy barrage, the *146e* and *153e Regiments d'infanterie* went over the top from their trenches on the eastern edge of Bois Favière and managed to cover the open ground to the village with relative ease. However, once they had entered the village, intense fighting ensued as the French tried to winkle the German defenders out of their deeply entrenched positions. Much underground fighting also took place as the defenders had interlinked many of the cellars in the houses of the village with a system of tunnels and turned the place - church, crypt and catacombs - into a veritable fortress. However, after two hours of fierce hand-to-hand fighting, the French had managed to capture the village and begun to dig in on the eastern outskirts, where the line would become static for a few weeks.

Once in Hardecourt-aux-Bois, take the right fork at the village war memorial (direction Guillemont) and keep right at the next junction. At the village church, take the left fork towards Guillemont and continue to the Y junction some 200 metres beyond the village boundary. At this junction is a wrought iron calvary set between four trees, a memorial to **Capitaine Augustin Cochin (6)**. *From here, there is a decent view westwards and south westwards towards the start line of 8 July and the final line of 1 July, Bois Favière.*

Capitaine Augustin Cochin's memorial.

Born in Paris on 22nd December 1876, Augustin Denis Marie Cochin was a social historian and author of several books on the French Revolution. An officer of the reserve, he was mobilised in August 1914 and, during his service, was made a chevalier of the *Légion d'honneur* and won the *Croix de guerre* with four palms. Wounded three times during his service (at Fouquesecourt on 25 September 1914, at Tahure on 25 September 1915 and at Douaumont on 26 February 1916), each time he returned to duty whilst still recovering from his injuries. Augustin was killed in action by a rifle bullet to the head in front of the calvary at Hardecourt aux Bois whilst his unit (*9e Compagnie, 3e Bataillon, 146e Regiment d'infanterie*) was assaulting the German positions in this vicinity on 8 July 1916. He has no known grave, although he is remembered on four separate memorials, including this one near to the spot where he fell and one where he studied (Chartres). Augustin's brother, Jaques - a *capitaine* in the *325e Régiment d'infanterie*, was also a chevalier of the *Légion d'honneur*. He was killed in action at Xon, Lorraine, in 1915.

The cross of this memorial was designed to represent weapons of war, such as machine gun belts and shells and, at the centre, is a representation of a soldier being carried to heaven within the wings of an angel. The gold painted inscription translates as: The more difficult the ordeal, the more necessary it is to be there. Here fell Captain Augustin Cochin, killed in the attack of 8 July 1916. Wounded three times, and with his arm broken, though disabled, he returned to the battle for the love of his country and his soldiers.

*Turn left at this junction (towards the site of Maltz Horn Farm, marked by a crucifix, and Trônes Wood) and travel a further 380 metres to the small junction with a farm track [it is possible to turn around here]. About 60 metres down this track, in the field to the left, is a small memorial (7) to **Marcel Boucher** and **Romeo Lepage** of the 153e Régiment d'infanterie, who were killed here together on 28 July 1916 when this location formed part of the front line.*

Soldat 2.Cl. Marcel Boucher, from Paris, was born on 13 May 1896 and *caporal* Roméo René

The memorial to Marcel Boucher and Romeo Lepage is located against a backdrop of the ground fought over on 8 July.

Octave Jules Lepage, a bank clerk in civilian life, was born at Vert-St Denis, Melun, just over a month later, on 20 June 1896. Though *classe de 1916*, both men had their compulsory military service dates brought forward due to the war and attested in April 1915. Seeing front line service as from October 1915, Marcel was a Verdun veteran who had seen action in the Haudromont Quarries and on Côte 304 between February and April 1916; Roméo, who had initially served in the *82e Regiment d'infanterie*, saw much action in the Argonne. Roméo transferred to the *153e Regiment d'infanterie* in March 1916 and was promoted to *caporal* on 13 July 1916, just fifteen days before his death. Both men's remains were lost during the fighting, but Marcel's were found and identified post war. These were repatriated to his family in Paris for private burial in November 1921. Roméo was never identified.

*Return to Hardecourt-aux-Bois and continue through the village to the first junction, Turn right and then immediate left towards Maricourt. This road takes you alongside **Bois sans Nom (8)** – nowadays known as Bois Brûle. At the point that the road starts to run alongside the wood, at a Y junction with a small track, stop. This is the exact point where the French front line crossed the road at the end of the first day. To the right (north), you will see the portion of Bois Favièr that was attacked and captured by the 146e Régiment d'infanterie and, to the left, Bois d'En-Haut, which was captured by the 1er bataillon of the 156e Régiment d'infanterie. The end of the day front line ran along the western edge of Bois Favièr, through your current location and along the northern edge of Bois d'En-Haut.*

An objective of the *2e Bataillon* of the *156e Régiment d'infanterie* on 1 July 1916, **Bois sans Nom** (and its quarry) had been completely captured and cleared by 8.30am, an hour after Zero Hour. The two attacking battalions (the *1er bataillon* was tasked with the capture of Bois d'En-Haut, to the south east of your location), reinforced by the *3e bataillon,* spent the remainder of the day consolidating their positions before successfully fending off two strong German counter-attacks in the early hours of 2 July and held the newly won positions until relieved on 4 July. Casualties had been light for the regiment during the operations of the 1 July – twenty two dead and 132 wounded across all three battalions.

Once the wood has been left, the road continues through the open fields traversed by the 156e Régiment d'infanterie and, as the Bois de Maricourt is neared, by the 26e régiment d'infanterie on 1 July 1916. Just before the point where the Bois de Maricourt touches the road, the

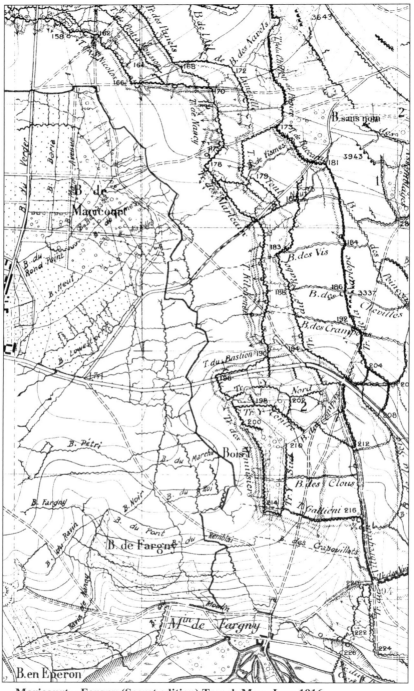

Maricourt – Fargny (Secret edition) Trench Map, June 1916.

French start line crossed the road. The start line for the 156e and 146e Régiments d'infanterie ran just in front of the western side of the wood to the north. The road upon which you are travelling was the centre of the 26e Régiment d'infanterie's area and the battalion demarcation line.

*At the D938, turn right and then right again onto the D197 and into the eastern part of **Maricourt** (9).*

A front line village up to July 1916, Maricourt was the junction between the British and French armies on the first day of the Battle of the Somme, with the French Army being in possession of the eastern half. Protected from direct view from the German lines by the Bois de Maricourt to the east, it was exposed to the north but still served as divisional headquarters for the *39e Division d'infanterie* and Brigade Headquarters for the *219e brigade* on the opening day. Its exposure, however, forced all French artillery units to be located south of the village.

*Continue on the D197through the outskirts of the village. After one kilometre, the flagpoles of the **Franco-British Memorial (10)** are reached. Turn right onto this side road (the Chemin des Anglais), noting the view towards Bois Favière in the near distance.*

The Anglo-French memorial at Maricourt marking the the front line location where the armies of the two nations joined and advanced together on 1 July.

103

Erected by the Somme Remembrance Association in November 2010, the memorial marks the location at which the French and the British lines met and consists of two flagpoles, one displaying the French Tricolore and the other flying the Union Flag, and an information panel. In French and English, the panel explains the history of the site and, along with a 1916 trench map extract, also displays the regimental insignia of the two units in occupation at this point on 1 July: the 17th (Service) Battalion (1st City) The King's (Liverpool) Regiment and the *3e bataillon, 153e Regiment d'infanterie*.

The actual junction with the British line is at this exact spot. Here, the line ran at a ninety degrees angle to the main road (D197) and continued down the *Chemin des Anglais* to the north-east corner of Bois de Maricourt, where it turned southwards, following the eastern edge of the wood.

The Anglo-French memorial.

Walk or drive to the north eastern corner of the Bois de Maricourt and look northwards (it is possible to turn a car around at this spot).

To your left, between this point and the main road, the *153e Regiment d'infanterie* launched their attack alongside the 1st Liverpool Pals (on the far side of the road) at 7.30am on 1 July, with the two battalion commanders, Lieutenant Colonel Bryan Charles Fairfax and *Chef de bataillon* Louis Gabriel Lepetit, advancing together in a show of solidarity between the two nations. Attacking due north, they had overrun the German front line within twenty minutes and broken through to take their objective to the rear of the German First Line (the *Tranchée des Framboises*) some 900 metres to the north. Following the capture of the first lines, elements of the regiment moved in a north-easterly direction (alongside and within the *Tranchée des Calottes)* towards the northern section of Bois Favière (viewable to your north east) in co-operation with the *146e Regiment d'infanterie,* where they encountered extremely stiff resistance and engaged in hand-to-hand combat amongst the trees. Tasked with the complete capture of this section of the wood, the defence was so tenacious that the line captured had to be consolidated within the north eastern corner of the wood at the end of the day, falling short of the objective by some seventy metres. This was one of only two locations on the battlefield where the French failed to complete their first day objectives.

To your right (and rear), the *146e Regiment d'infanterie* attacked from the Bois de Maricourt in a north-easterly direction towards the southern and mid sections of Bois Favière. Within twenty minutes they had penetrated into the wood and taken their objective (the eastern edge of the wood) a short while later, where they consolidated their position and successfully repulsed a strong German counter-attack during the late afternoon. As a point of note, the regimental history of the *146e* mentions that the artillery preparation had been extremely effective in the southern section of the wood, yet was insufficient in the north, perhaps accounting for the failure to capture all the objectives in this area. Casualties for the *153e* and *146e Regiments d'infanterie* during the assault on Bois Favière amounted to 159 (with thirty six dead) and 282 (fifty five fatalities) respectively.

GPS Waypoints, Tour 1 Part 1

1 - 49°56'57.88"N, 2°45'57.03"E   2 - 49°56'20.34"N, 2°46'48.08"E
3 - 49°58'1.73"N, 2°48'13.08"E   4 - 49°57'52.12"N, 2°48'54.08"E
5 - 49°59'23.39"N, 2°49'0.28"E   6 - 49°59'38.49"N, 2°49'12.61"E
7 - 49°59'46.85"N, 2°48'56.24"E   8 - 49°59'12.17"N, 2°48'26.61"E
9 - 49°58'47.26"N, 2°47'21.14"E   10 - 49°59'15.04"N, 2°47'27.70"E

Tour 1: North of the Somme
Part 2 – The continuing battle:
July – August

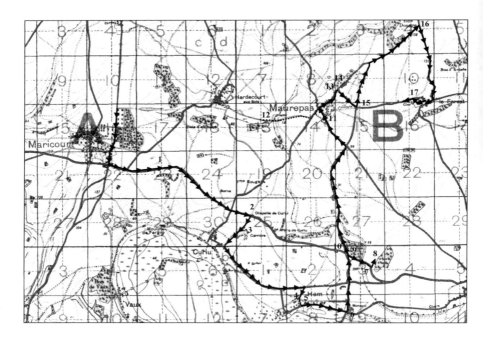

Return down the same road towards Maricourt and turn left onto the D938. After just under a kilometre, a memorial (1) can be seen in a hedged enclosure on the left. Stop here.

Though this memorial is dedicated to an action at this spot from 1914, and therefore outside the scope of this book, it is, being located on the position of German front line of 1 July 1916, a worthwhile viewpoint for the 1 July actions of the *69e Regiment d'infanterie*.

The memorial itself is dedicated to the ***224e Regiment d'infanterie*** and their unsuccessful attack on Hardecourt aux Bois at 7.05am on 17 December 1914 in which, after coming under heavy fire almost instantly after leaving their positions in front of Maricourt, three officers and fifty

The memorial commemorating *Lieutenant* Robert Brodu and the actions of the *224e Régiment d'infanterie* on 17 December 1914. This monument also marks the location of the German front line captured by the *69e Regiment d'infanterie*, with no fatalities, on 1 July 1916.

eight men were killed and 263 wounded. Specifically, it commemorates *Lieutenant* **Robert Brodu**, who was one of the officers killed that day.

Born in Paris on 30 March 1881, Marie Joseph Jules Robert Brodu was the commanding officer of the *20e compagnie, 5e bataillon, 224e Regiment d'infanterie*. He was killed, along with his second in command and all of the section commanders, near this spot within minutes of the start of the attack on 17 December 1914. The memorial translates as:

To the memory of Lt Robert Brodu Legion d'Honneur, Croix de Guerre. Commanding the 20th Company of the 224th Infantry Regiment and the officers, NCOs and soldiers who fell with him during the attack of 17 December 1914

The main road itself lies in the centre of the attack of the *69e Regiment d'infanterie,* who advanced either side of it on 1 July. Looking beyond the hedge of the memorial towards Maricourt, they attacked from their start positions some 100 metres away and towards and through your present location (the German front line) to a point, across the open fields,

1200 metres to the east. Advancing behind a violent rolling barrage (a creeping barrage in British parlance), they encountered deserted trenches and destroyed positions and strongpoints in their advance through the German first line of defence. All objectives were taken, with very light casualties. Fifteen men were wounded in this attack, with no deaths, though a further eight were evacuated as sick during the consolidation period later in the day.

*Continue for a further two kilometres, past the first crossroads, marking the limit of the first day advance of the 79e and 37e Regiments d'infanterie, and turn right towards Curlu at the **Chapelle de Curlu (2).***

The Chapelle de Curlu – reconstructed on the same spot as the original, this was regularly utilised as an artillery reference point by both sides throughout the Battle of the Somme.

A chapel, the *Notre Dame de Pitié*, has existed on this site from 1410 and it is said that it was here that King Charles VI stopped to pray during the Armagnac-Burgundian Civil War whilst en route to fight the Burgundians at Bapaume in July 1414. Though this chapel is a reconstruction, the original structure – though damaged – survived the July 1916 fighting and was used as an artillery reference point at varying times.

Heading back into Curlu, one of the old Curlu phosphate quarries, the
carrière de Eulenbourg (3), *is passed on the left.*

The carrière de Eulenbourg, marking the limit of the advance of the *37e Régiment d'infanterie* to the north-east of Curlu on 1 July, was a German strongpoint and the location of one of the machine gun positions that slowed up the capture of the village. It was captured by the *2e bataillon, 37e Régiment d'infanterie* following a heavy bombardment in the early evening of the 1st.

Turn left at the first junction.

On the left, in the field, you will see Bois du 80 before the road skirts a wooded area, the rear of which is called Bois de Gimble, concealing the remains of another phosphate quarry. Yet another quarry, carrière Span, can be found in the woodland to the right immediately after the Gimble woodland. These were all defensive positions in 1916, with the carrière Span being a heavily entrenched location containing a fortified machine gun position covering the approach to the village of Hem **(4)**. These areas were captured by the *37e Régiment d'infanterie*, reinforced by two companies of the *79e Régiment d'infanterie* and three dismounted *peletons* of the *5e hussards* when, after slight adjustments in position and minor advances between 2 and 4 July, operations in the area resumed on the 5th.

*Continue over the crossroads and take the next right into **Hem** village.*

Captured by the aforementioned units on 5 July, the French were expecting to have a tougher time in capturing this village than they had for Curlu. Defended by thick wire defences, interspaced with the defended quarries and small woodlands that you have just passed, the capture of this village, and the Hem Plateau to the north, was designed to clear the area of the German artillery that was harassing the *16e* and *2e Divisions d'infanterie coloniale* located south of the river.

Following a heavy bombardment, the *37e Régiment d'infanterie* attacked under the cover of a river fog at 6.58am on 5 July and, after clearing the quarries and woods, moved towards Hem. By 8.15am the objectives north of the village had been gained; but the village itself would require a further heavy bombardment and another nine hours of vicious fighting until it was completely cleared and the *79e Régiment d'infanterie* was in occupation of the Bois du Fromage, immediately to its east.

The advance was stopped to the east of the village by the strong German defences situated in the vicinity of Monacu and, to the north and north-east, by positions situated along the Péronne road and in another quarry and farm buildings (Ferme de la Carrière) in front of Bois de Hem. A number of German counter-attacks were fended off and close quarter fighting took place in Bois du Sommet and Bois de l'Observation as the Germans managed to regain a small portion of territory on the Hem Plateau over the next twenty four hours and attained even more up to 12 July: the woods of du Sommet, de l'Observation and du Fromage changed hands no less than five times between 5 and 7 July The result was that the line was moved slightly southwards and towards the village.

The next major action at Hem took place on 20 July following the relief of the *11e* and *29e Divisions d'infanterie* by the *153e* and *47e*. During this action, the *2e Brigade des chasseurs alpins* (commanded by *Colonel* Maurice Gamelin of 1940 fame) of the *47e Division d'infanterie* fought through and recaptured Bois du Sommet and Bois de l'Observation; and the division then cleared the Hem Plateau as far as the Ferme de la Carrière, basically recapturing the ground lost between 5 and 12 July and taking over 600 prisoners in the process. However, the area east of Hem village and the Monacu farm buildings still remained firmly in German hands.

*At the first crossroads, **Hem-Monacu multi-unit memorial (5)** commemorates the 30th July 1916 actions of the 6e Armée, 7e Corps d'Armée , 41e Division d'infanterie, 82e Brigade d'infanterie, 23e Régiment d'infanterie, 133e Régiment d'infanterie, 229e Régiment d'infanterie, 2e Régiment mixte de zouaves et tirailleurs, 2 Division de cavalerie and the 10e Groupe de Auto-Mitrailleuses-Autos-Canons. This is located to the left of the church. Next to this memorial there is an associated information panel describing the actions of this day. There is also a plaque dedicated to the memory of the **23e regiment d'infanterie**, which is located on the wall of the village mairie.*

*Continue through the crossroads to the T junction. From here, a visit to Hem Farm British cemetery can be made, if desired, by turning right and continuing for 600 meters. If not, turn left and continue to the junction with the D146. The buildings to your left front are the current incarnation of **Monacu Ferme (6)**.*

A German strongpoint that had managed to withstand the assaults of 5 and 20 July 1916 (along with smaller scale local operations on 27 and 28 July), the area opposite was held by troops of the *41e Division*

The multi-unit memorial at Hem commemorating the *6e Armée* actions here on 30 July 1916.

The formidable and heavily fortified Monacu Farm. The target of several costly assaults (including one cross-river assault), heavily bombarded and soaked with gas, the farm never fell to direct military action as the Germans eventually abandoned the position.

d'infanterie by the last week of the month. A new attack was scheduled for 30 July and the area of Monacu and the north was heavily shelled and soaked with gas on the 29th in preparation. At 4.45am on the 30th, the attack was launched but proved to be a disaster. All along the line from the river to the area north of Bois de Hem the advancing French soldiers were caught in a terrific crossfire of machine guns and German defensive artillery fire. Communications broke down, with cables being severed by artillery and the continuous assault line was broken into isolated units. All along the front units were forced back to their start line.

At Monacu Ferme, however, the *229e Régiment d'infanterie*, reinforced by the *2e Régiment mixte de zouaves et tirailleurs* who, after crossing the bridge over the Somme from Feuillières, attacked from the south, managed to break through at the T junction immediately north of the farm. They were, however, beaten back later in the day. Following a bombardment on 1 August, another attempt was made and trenches to the north were captured in the evening. During a continuing barrage on the farm, the Germans decided to vacate the position and, by 3am on 3 August, the *19e compagnie, 229e Régiment d'infanterie* were in occupation of the ruins.

Turn left, and head north on the D146 until you reach the intersection with the D938

Here, you are roughly following the German front line of 30 July 1916. It was in these fields to your left that (from the south, heading northwards) the 229e, 133e and 23e Régiments d'infanterie were so badly hit during their assault on this date.

As you approach the intersection with the D938, look to the left.

In the field between your present location and the trees some 300 metres distant, used to stand the **ferme de la Carrière.** The trees you now see are hiding are the remains of another of the ubiquitous phosphate quarries. Bois du Sommet and Bois de l'Observation lay beyond this quarry, but are no longer in existence.

Turn right here at the intersection onto the D938 towards Pèronne. After 500 meters (just after the motorway bridge has been crossed) note the **monument to the 363e Régiment d'infanterie (7)** *on the left.*

The *363e Régiment d'infanterie* (the reserve regiment of the *163e Régiment d'infanterie*) was formed at Nice on 2 August 1914. Part of the

Memorial to the *363e Régiment d'infanterie* at the entrance to the Nécropole nationale de Cléry-sur Somme.

41e Division d'infanterie from 1914-1917, it saw service in the Vosges before arriving on the Somme in mid-July 1916. On 1 August, the *363e* relieved the *133e Régiment d'infanterie* in the Bois de Hem sector and took part in the attack on the wood and on the *tranchée de Bois du Ver* on 7 August. Later actions on the Somme included attacks on the Cléry – Maurepas road and the *tranchée de Terline* before the regiment left the Somme in September. During the Battle of the Somme (their first major battle and one in which they spent just ten days at the front) the *363e* suffered some 1,282 casualties.

Turn left at this monument and continue up the track to the **Nécropole nationale de Cléry-sur Somme (8)**

Originally known as the *cimetière militaire français du bois des Ouvrages*, the cemetery was named after the finger shaped wood (Earthworks Copse to the British) that once stood on the site of the trees that now shield the cemetery from the A1 motorway to the west. The wood on to which the cemetery backs is the **Bois Croisette**.

Created in 1920 from a concentration of cemeteries and individual graves around the sectors of Monacu Farm, Fargny and the Bois de Berlingots, it also contains French graves from the communal cemeteries of the communes of Morlancourt and Vaires-sous-Corbie. There are the remains of 2,332 French soldiers buried here, with 1,129 contained within two ossuaries and of whom 1,062 in total are unknown.

Not one of the most heavily defended woodlands on the Somme, given that it lay between two German defensive lines, Bois Croisette was

The *Nécropole nationale de Cléry-sur Somme* with Bois Croisette in the background.

captured during the advance of 3 September that was launched in conjunction with the British attacks further north (the Battle of Guillemont).

*Return to the D938 and turn right. In 500 metres (the same junction as before), turn right onto the D146 and, immediately the road is surrounded by **Bois de Hem** (9).*

Between 20 and 30 July, the western edge of Bois de Hem had become the front line in this area, with the road upon which you are now travelling marking the German forward trench. During the disastrous attacks of 30 July, the *23e Régiment d'infanterie* managed to break through the German lines and enter the wood on its southern edge (along the D938), whilst other elements were being held up in front of the German defences on the western edge of the wood. Although eventually beaten back, they did manage, in one of the rare successes of that day, to advance the line some 400 metres and to hold their new position until relieved on the night of the 2/3 August. However, they suffered some 519 casualties in this feat, 106 of whom were killed and 196 missing.

Fighting continued in and in front of the wood into August, with the *363e Régiment d'infanterie* launching a successful assault on the *tranchée de Bois du Ver,* which ran vertically through the centre of the wood (parts

114

of this trench can still be located within the wood today) on 7 August. The units of the *41e Division d'infanterie* in the wood were relieved by those of the *14e Division d'infanterie* on 10 August who, in cooperation with the *47e Division d'infanterie*, during local attacks on the 12, 13, 16, 18 and 24 August finally pushed the Germans out of the wood – the *66e Division d'infanterie* taking over and continuing the push on Cléry on 25 August.

Upon entering the wooded area, you will see the mysterious 'H.R.' memorial **(10)** *on the left. It is in the fields behind this memorial where the unsuccessful assault of 30 July was broken up.*

A simple stele inscribed with the details '**H.R. 12 août 1916**', the identity of the person who this memorial commemorates has been the subject of some online debate since about 2012. It would appear, from the evidence supplied by volunteers from memorialgenweb.org and members of the pages14-18.com discussion forum, that the identity of 'H.R.' is almost certainly that of **H**enri **R**ayssiguier.

The mysterious 'H.R.' memorial in Bois de Hem. Located at the 'v' in the road once the wood has been entered, this memorial can be easily missed.

Henri Joseph Rayssiguier was a *Soldat 2e classe* in the *170e Régiment d'infanterie* at the time of his death (13 August 1916). He was born at Le Pradal, Hérault, on 1 August 1885 and was a farmer in his civilian life. He was called up for his compulsory military service at Bézieres on 7 October 1905 and served with the *17e Régiment d'infanterie* during this period, seeing service in Tunisia between 1907 and 1908. On 21 September 1908, Henri returned to civilian life (but was refused a good conduct certificate upon his demobilisation!) but continued to serve as a reservist. Called back into service on 2 August 1914, he initially trained with the *163e Régiment d'infanterie* before transferring to the *111e Régiment d'infanterie* in October 1914. He was transferred yet again prior to active service and arrived at the front with the *174e Régiment d'infanterie* at the end of June 1915 as part of a replacement draft for their horrendous losses in the Artois battles. Wounded in action on the Aisne on 4 September 1915 (gunshot wound to the left upper arm), it can be assumed that his transfer to the *170e Régiment d'infanterie* occurred following his recovery from this injury. Henri's service record mentions no further transfers after the *174e*, yet his 'mort pour la France' fiche and grave records all state that he was in the *170e* at the time of his death. To further muddy the waters, both the *170e* and *174e* were serving in this area at the same time, both being part of the *48e Division d'infanterie*. The *48e Division* was in action east and north east of Monacu Ferme during the advance on Cléry on 12 and 13 August 1916. Henri was one of the casualties of this action and is now buried in the *Nécropole nationale de Cléry-sur Somme* (grave number 127).

*Continue northwards on the D146 for 2.25 kilometres - crossing the area between the German second main defensive line and a subsidiary 'river defensive' line that was assaulted and captured during the operatoions of 12 to 13 August - and take a left turn at the crossroads to approach the western side of **Maurepas** (11).*

A fortified village on the German Second Line (and the hinge between it and Second Subsidiary Line), Maurepas was directly assaulted on 30 July, 12 August, 18 August and 24 August 1916. Though the 30 July attack was an abject failure, the attack of the 12th, which had been preceded by an intense artillery bombardment, succeeded in forcing the Germans back to the north eastern half of the village. Here, with practically every building covered by machine guns, they held out for another week. On 19 August French artillery once again concentrated on Maurepas, destroying most of what was left of the buildings and eradicating the trenches in and around the village. However, many of the subterranean

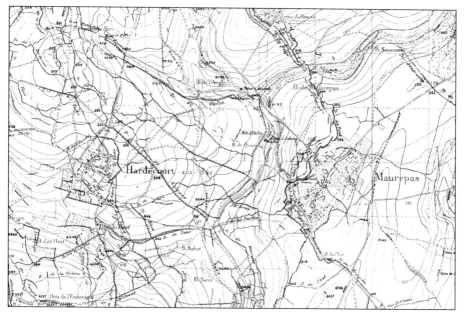

Hardecourt – Maurepas Trench Map, 16 August 1916.

shelters and emplacements survived this bombardment and it was not
until 24 August attack that the village finally fell completely into the
possession of the *1e Division d'infanterie*.

Turn right at the crossroads onto the D146b into the centre of the village.

Optional Diversion: The Chomet memorial (12)

*If desired, a short detour can be made here by turning left instead of right.
Follow the right fork after 200 metres and, on the left verge after 850
metres, you will come across the memorial to **Soldat 2.Cl.Gaston Chomet**
of the 160e Régiment d'infanterie, who was killed near this spot on 30
July 1916.*

Born at Saint Donat, Auvergne on 19 March 1895, Gaston was enlisted
into the *160e Régiment d'infanterie* at Versailles on 9 September 1915.
After serving at the front from April 1916 and taking part in the fighting
at Verdun, he arrived on the Somme in May 1916. His regiment was in
reserve on 1 July 1916, but moved into the front line on 3/4 July near
Bois sans Nom and played a role in the capture of Hardecourt-aux-Bois
on the 8th before moving out of the line for a rest. Gaston was killed

Memorial to *Soldat 2.Cl.* Gaston Chomet of the *160e Régiment d'infanterie* near Maurepas.

during the failed attempt to capture the village of Maurepas during the disastrous attacks of 30 July 1916. His grave location is unrecorded.

End of Diversion.

At Maurepas green/sports field there are memorials at either side of it - the village war memorial and the memorial to the **9e Regiment de Zouaves (13)** at the western end and, on the eastern end, a memorial to the **1er Régiment d'infanterie (14),** who were both involved in the attacks on Maurepas around the areas between the church and the village cemetery. The *9e Regiment de Zouaves* were in action here on 12 and 18 August and the *1er Régiment d'infanterie* on the 12th and 24th, when they pushed through the village and on to the *tranchée Brody*, some 900 metres beyond.

Memorial erected by
veterans of the *9e
Regiment de Zouaves*,
who fought in this area
during the Somme
offensive and in
particular here in
Maurepas on 12 and 18
August.

*Turn right at the centre of the green (signposted A1 and Feuillèrs). After 600 metres, the **Nécropole nationale de Maurepas** (15) is reached.*

The **Nécropole nationale de Maurepas** was created in 1916 while the Battle of the Somme was still in progress. In 1921 and 1936 it was expanded by the concentration of remains from two smaller cemeteries at Suzanne and the western side of Maurepas, along with those from isolated graves near Albert. Presently the cemetery contains the remains of 3,657 French soldiers (including 1,588 buried within two ossuaries),

The Nécropole nationale de Maurepas.

one French civilian, one Romanian and nineteen Russians. The Russians and the Romanian were prisoners of war and members of German work battalions who mainly died between late December 1916 and the spring of 1917.

Leave the cemetery and return to Maurepas. Turn right at the junction with the D146 towards Combles. After 1,900 metres (the next road junction), the **Memorial to Victor Hallard (16)** *is to be found on the right.*

Memorial to *Soldat 1er classe* **Victor Hallard of the** *110e Régiment d'infanterie.*

Soldat 1er classe Victor Hallard was born in Paris on 12 May 1888. A recalled reservist in August 1914, he was serving in the *110e Régiment d'infanterie* at the time he was killed in action on 12 September 1916. Victor was killed near to (and buried at) this spot – one of 267 deaths from his regiment on this day – during an attack on this crossroads whilst attempting to break through to le Priez ferme and Rancourt. It is unclear as to whether Victor's remains are still buried here or whether they were returned for private burial.

Erected by his parents, the memorial states that he was also known as 'Tredez'.

Take the small road to the right towards Le Forest. Looking over to your right, through the small valley, you will see the path of the attack of the 43e Bataillon de chasseurs à pied in their attack of 3 September 1916. After 1.75 kilometres, the tiny hamlet of **Le Forest (17)** *is reached.*

An attacker's eye view of the hamlet of Le Forest at the point where the main
German defensive line was breached on 3 September.

Part of an eastwards movement during a series of attacks between 3 and
5 September, the area of Le Forest was assaulted by the *2e* and *46e
Divisions d'infanterie*, with the *45e Divisions d'infanterie* joining the
fray to the immediate north of Le Forest the following day. Captured by
the *43e Bataillon de chasseurs à pied* at about 2pm on 3 September, the
Chasseurs had endured heavy German shelling whilst crossing the valley
between Maurepas and Le Forest and then cleared three intact trenches

The valley across which the *43e Bataillon de chasseurs à pied* advanced under
heavy fire in their assault from Maurepas to Le Forest on 3 September.

of their Prussian Guard occupants at bayonet point, capturing seven machine guns and taking nine officers, twenty-nine NCOs and 190 other ranks prisoner. Following the conquest of Le Forest, the advance continued to the Ferme de l'Hospital in the process of overrunning a couple of artillery batteries, where they endured several days of constant shelling. Receiving two regimental citations for these actions, the *Chasseurs* suffered sixty three dead, sixteen missing and 182 wounded in this action.

Follow the main road round past the small church. Once the western edge of Le Forest has been reached, look back towards Maurepas. You now have the view of the German defenders of Le Forest as the chasseurs advanced towards you. A major German trench line overlooked the valley some 150 metres to your front (tranchée de la Craniere on the left of the road and tranchée du Caucase on the right).

GPS Waypoints, Tour 1 Part 2

1 - 49°58'36.98"N, 2°48'5.37"E	2 - 49°58'9.47"N, 2°49'33.77"E
3 - 49°57'58.39"N, 2°49'19.31"E	4 - 49°57'26.37"N, 2°49'45.85"E
5 - 49°57'18.89"N, 2°50'18.88"E	6 - 49°57'12.32"N, 2°51'3.42"E
7 - 49°57'40.74"N, 2°51'27.32"E	8 - 49°57'46.32"N, 2°51'33.06"E
9 - 49°57'46.06"N, 2°51'2.87"E	10 - 49°57'48.89"N, 2°50'59.44"E
11 - 49°59'10.89"N, 2°50'41.04"E	12 - 49°59'8.21"N, 2°49'47.31"E
13 - 49°59'26.19"N, 2°50'49.43"E	14 - 49°59'28.77"N, 2°50'51.61"E
15 - 49°59'16.35"N, 2°51'9.83"E	16 - 50° 0'7.86"N, 2°52'3.25"E
17 - 49°59'21.21"N, 2°52'13.33"E	

Tour 1: North of the Somme
Part 3 – The continuing battle:
September – November

Turn around and return up the road you have just travelled. After 400 meters, turn right (under the TGV line and motorway) and then take an immediate right. At the road junction, after 500 metres, look to your left.

At the top of the crest is **Ferme de l'Hôpital (1)**, an important observation post and the location of three German artillery batteries and another of the *2e* and *26e Divisions d'infanterie* objectives of the 3 -5 September actions.

*Continue straight on at the junction for a further 500 meters and another road junction. In the field on your left is a monument to **Caporal-fourier Edouard Naudier** of the 46e Régiment d'infanterie **(2)**, who died of his wounds at Ferme de l'Hôpital on 22 September 1916.*

A tax collector in civilian life, Edouard was born at Gastins, Seine et Marne, on 6 April 1890. He was incorporated into the *46e Régiment d'infanterie* on 9 October 1912 and was still serving at the time of the outbreak of war. A veteran of the Battle of the Marne in 1914, he fought in the Argonne throughout 1915 before arriving at the Somme in 1916. Wounded in the aftermath of a German attack near Bouchavesnes on 22 September 1916, Edouard died in the dressing station established near the farm later that same day. Initially buried in the small cemetery located at the farm, his grave was later lost.

*Continue down this road towards **Cléry sur Somme** (3).*

An objective during the August and September advances along the north bank of the river, **Cléry** was directly assaulted on 24 August 1916 by the *42e Régiment d'infanterie,* who lost over 600 men in the attempt. The village eventually fell to the *64e Bataillon de chasseurs à pied* and the *68e Bataillon de chasseurs Alpins* of the *66e Division d'infanterie* on 3 September 1916.

For the next two and a half kilometres, the road roughly follows the German front line of 4 September 1916 (which lay in the fields to the

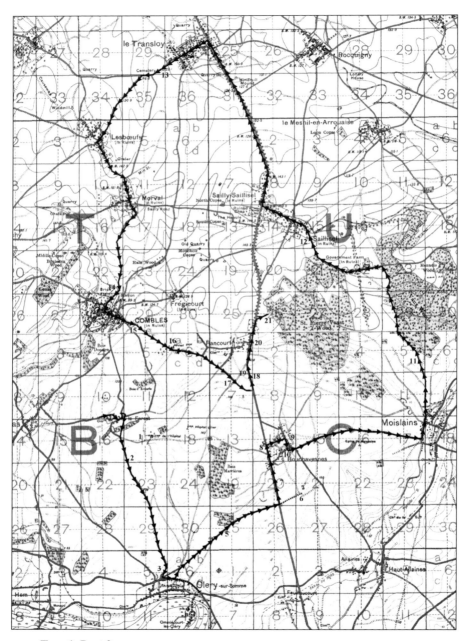

Tour 1, Part 3.

124

right). One of the trenches in this area was the *tranchée Fryatt*, named in honour of the British Merchant Navy captain who had been executed in Bruges by the Germans on 27 July 1916 for attempting to ram the U-33 in March 1915. This whole area was taken by the *66e Division d'infanterie* in the 3-5 September operation.

In Cléry, turn left onto the D938 and, after 300 metres turn left onto the D149.

Optional diversion: *Omiécourt-lès-Cléry*

*At this point it is possible to pay an optional visit across the river to the **memorial plaques at Omiécourt-lès-Cléry** (4) by continuing a further 500 metres and taking a right turn. 600 metres beyond this junction and over the river is the hamlet of Omiécourt-lès-Cléry. One of the first buildings on the right has three plaques on the wall…one commemorating the **9e Regiment de Cuirassiers a Pied and their liberation of Omiécourt on 5 September 1916**. The other two commemorate a local victim of Ravensbruck Concentration Camp (Anne-Marie Vion 1922-1945) and the veterans association of Cléry. Return back the same way to the road junction in Cléry.)*

Memorial plaques at Omiécourt-les-Cléry.

This is a rather beautiful area and there is seating in a small park by the river, making it an ideal picnic stop.
End of Diversion.

*Follow the D149 for 1.75km.and stop at the corner of the wood (**Bois Madame**).*

Bois Madame was one of three heavily defended woods forming part of the German Third Line (the others being Bois Marrières and Bois Reinette to the north) and one of the objectives of the *66e Division d'infanterie*. It was assaulted in textbook style and captured within three hours of the start of the attack.

*Here is the memorial to **Soldat 2e classe Gustav Fumery** of the 132e Régiment d'infanterie **(5)**, who was killed near here on the 4 October 1916.*

Gustave Fumery was born at Aire-sur-la-Lys, Pas-de-Calais, on 31 May 1896 and was a student at the time of the outbreak of war. He was incorporated into the *150e Régiment d'infanterie* on 9 April 1915 and, after serving on the Argonne

Memorial to *Soldat 2e classe Gustav Fumery* of the *132e Régiment d'infanterie* located in the corner of Bois Madame.

and Champagne fronts, transferred to the *132e Régiment d'infanterie* on 22 March 1916. With the *132e*, Gustave fought at Verdun before moving to the Somme. He was killed in action by a shell detonation 'near the Bouchavesnes – Bapaume road' on 4 October 1916 and buried in the small cemetery at the Bois Madame on 5 October. Later moved to the Nécropole nationale de Cléry-sur Somme, his remains were eventually reburied privately.

*The location also affords good views over the **Haute Montjoie Plateau** and of **Bois de Berlinval** and **Bois des Berlingots**, where some of the final actions of the Somme immediately north of the river took place: Bois de Berlingots marking the final extent of advance in this area.*

Captured by the *70e Division d'infanterie* on 12 September 1916 during an advance from the *Tranchée de Berlingots*, located on the western edge of Bois de Berlinval (the right hand wood as you look at it), Bois de Berlingots was only occupied for one night before a strong German

Bois de Berlingots

Bois de Berlinval

The Montjoie Plateau as viewed from Bois Madame. Bois Berlingots marked the limit of the French advance in this area and there was much ferocious fighting between the two woods during September 1916.

counter-attack pushed the French back to and beyond their start position. Retaken later in the day, this wood became a contested front line position for the remainder of the battle – a position rendered even more dangerous due to the incessant attention paid to it by the German guns located on Mont St Quentin, just north of Péronne.

*Continue a further 1,200 metres to the junction of the N17. Directly in front of you, across the road, is a track leading, after 400 metres, to the site of the heavily fortified **Ferme du Bois Labé** (6), which is also the location of the memorial commemorating **Aspirant Maurice Gallé** of the 106e Régiment d'infanterie. Though accessible to the public, it is not advised to drive a standard car up this track.*

Maurice Gallé was a student from Creil, Oise, who was born on 17 February 1895. He was called into service with the *150e Régiment d'infanterie* on 20 December 1914 and, soon after arriving on the Argonne front, was rapidly promoted to *caporal* and then to *sergent* in April 1915. Transferring to the *106e Régiment*

Aspirant **Maurice Gallé** , *106e Régiment d'infanterie.*

127

Maurice Gallé's memorial at Ferme du Bois Labé also doubles as a memorial to the soldiers from Bouchavesnes who fell during the war. Overseen by the German guns on Mont St Quentin, this was an extremely dangerous location from September 1916 through to and beyond the end of the Battle of Somme.

d'infanterie on 30 October 1915, he fought in the Champagne sector and then at Verdun before arriving on the Somme where, on 5th September 1916, Maurice was appointed *aspirant*. He was seen to fall after being wounded in the stomach and posted as missing in action near this spot on 25 September 1916 – his death only being officially recognised after the discovery of his remains by British soldiers in this sector on 28 February 1917.

Ferme du Bois Labé was captured by the *44e* and *133e Régiments d'infanterie* during the early hours of 13 September 1916, following on from the general attack on Bouchavesnes launched during the evening of the 12th. Like Bois de Berlingots, this position then formed the southern flank of the French Army north of the River Somme and was swept with artillery constantly. The next twenty days after the taking of this position were spent in reinforcing the shattered trenches and, rather than just making the location as habitable as possible, the priority was in making the position survivable. Ferme du Bois Labé would remain a front line position until the German withdrawal from the area in 1917.

At the junction, turn left onto the N17 (D1017), signposted to Bouchavesnes-Bergen and Moislains. After 350 metres, note the remains of an old quarry in the trees on the right **(7)**.

This quarry – once the location of two German artillery batteries - was taken and held by the *44e Régiment d'infanterie* between midnight and 4am on 13 September. It served as the jumping off point for them and the *133e Régiment d'infanterie* in their assault on Ferme du Bois Labé later that same morning.

After a further 800 metres a **statue of** *Maréchal* **Ferdinand Foch (8)** *will be seen on the left.*

Commemorating the capture of Bouchavesnes by the French on 12 September 1916 and by the British on 1 September 1918 (the statue depicts Foch in his 1918 role as a *Maréchal* and *Généralissime* of Allied forces on the Western Front), this monument was the gift of Norwegian businessman, Haakon Wallem, who asked Foch which place he considered was the most significant to the French on the Somme. After replying 'Bouchavesnes', Wallem arranged for the statue to be erected here. Unveiled on 4 July 1926, the statue was sculpted by Firmin Michelet (who also sculpted the statue of Foch at Rethondes and, like Foch himself,

Statue of *Maréchal***, and** *Généralissime* **of Allied forces, Ferdinand Foch, commemorating both the French and British actions of 1916 and 1918 near this location on the main Bapaume – Péronne road at Bouchavesnes**

129

was born in Tarbes). In 1920, in honour of Wallem and his assistance in gaining funds from Norway to help in its post-war reconstruction, the village of Bouchavesnes added the name of his birthplace to its title, becoming Bouchavesnes-Bergen. There is a plaque to Wallem on the village school.

Take the next right into **Bouchavesnes-Bergen (9)**, *past the cemetery and to a T junction.*

Bouchavesnes was the easternmost village captured during the Battle of the Somme. The southern part was taken by the *44e* and *133e Régiments d'infanterie* and the north by the *6e Brigade de chasseurs,* under the command of the former French Minister of War, *Colonel* Adolphe Messimy. In an advance in which over three kilometres of ground and a length of the German Third Line was gained, the ruins of the village fell to the French in the evening of 12 September 1916. The road into the village that you have just travelled marks the route of the advance of the *28e Bataillon de chasseurs Alpin* as they attacked (without orders) into the village.

Turn right at this junction and pass the church (noting the town war memorial in front). On the southern corner of the church is a **memorial to the 91e Régiment d'infanterie (10)**.

A regiment that had seen action since the early days of the war, the *91e Régiment d'infanterie* fought through the Battles of the Frontiers, Lorraine and the Marne in 1914. 1915 saw them in action in the Argonne, on the Wöevre, Les Éparges, the Champagne and then back again to the Argonne, where they remained until their arrival on the Somme in September 1916. They were heavily engaged in the Bouchavesnes/Bois Saint-Pierre Vaast sector in October 1916, hence the location of their memorial.

Turn left onto the D149 and follow the road to **Moislains.**

Memorial commemorating the *91e Régiment d'infanterie* **by Bouchavesnes church.**

Behind the German lines during the entire Battle of the Somme, Moislains was a relatively safe area of respite for German troops until the September 1916 advances. The location of numerous headquarters and depots, it featured prominently during the *Bataille de Péronne* of 28 – 30 August 1914 when, at dawn on the 28th, patrols from the *20e Régiment de dragons* were surprised by the German troops holding Moislains. As the morning mist cleared, the French, including the *307e* and *308e Régiments d'infanterie* from Charente, came under heavy fire from the Germans in and around the village in the vicinity of Bois de Vaux and Bois Saint Pierre Vaast. After sustaining heavy losses, a withdrawal ensued in the early afternoon; however, the pursuing Germans were themselves hit badly and stopped by the French artillery located at Mesnil-en-Arrouaise. Casualties were very high, with the *307e Régiment d'infanterie* losing 1,700 (killed wounded and missing), with a further 1,300 from the *308e Régiment d'infanterie*.

At the first junction in Moislains, turn left towards the town centre and go straight ahead at the first cross roads after 350 metres. After a further 100 metres, take the left fork at the Y junction and then the central road (of three) at the next (direction Sailly-Saillisel). In one kilometre, you will arrive at the **Cimetière militaire de Moislains (11)** *on the right.*

Better known as the *Cimetière des Charentais*, this small cemetery was begun by the Germans in August 1914 following the 'Combat de Moislains'. Containing the remains of 465 soldiers (mainly from the *307e* and *308e Régiments d'infanterie* of 28th August 1914), 366 of the fallen

The *Cimetière des Charentais* near Moislains. Constructed by the German Army for the French fallen of August 1914 this almost 'regimental' cemetery was slightly extended in the 1920s but, heavily reminiscent of the battlefield cemeteries of the Franco-German War of 1870-71, still retains its character to this day.

The ossuary of the *Cimetière des Charentais* as it appeared in 1915.

are buried in an ossuary at the rear, marked by a monument to these regiments. Unusually for a French military cemetery, there are a number of original headstones still to be seen.

From here, continue on the road to Sailly-Saillisel, skirting Bois des Vaux. Over the fields to the left is the rear of Bois Saint Pierre Vaast.

Funnelled into the open ground by these two woods, the French infantry were cut down in swathes in the field to your left as they moved on Moislains on 28 August 1914. It was also here that the French artillery managed to stop the German pursuit as the Germans themselves entered this killing ground.

*Follow the road, skirting the northern part of Bois Saint Pierre Vaast, past Le Gouvernement Ferme and on to **Sailly-Saillisel** (12).*

Marking the northernmost extreme of the French sector of the Somme at the end of the 1916 battle, the attacks to capture Sailly-Saillisel began on October 6 1916. With the *150e* and *161e Régiments d'infanterie* facing the village directly, the *154e* and *135e Régiments d'infanterie* to their immediate right and the British Army to their left, the attack was preceded by a diversionary assault on Bois Saint Pierre Vaast. Launched at 2pm, the French advanced through the *Tranchées de Carlsbad, Tirpitz* and *Berlin* and captured the heavily defended *ouvrage de Tripot* and its nearby

wood before taking the western side of Sailly-Saillisel and its ruined
chateau. Here, the advance was halted and positions were consolidated
in preparation for the next phase.

On the night of 15/16 October, the *6e compagnie* of the *150e Régiment
d'infanterie* advanced into the houses of Sailly-Saillisel and moved across
the Bapaume road. House to house fighting began in earnest and, though
heavily defended, inch by inch the village began to fall into French hands.
On 18 October the *150e Régiment d'infanterie* and 9e *Régiment
d'zouaves* made a combined push and, by the early hours of 19 October,
practically the whole village was under French occupation, though it
would take until 29 October to totally clear the Germans. After defending
against several counter-attacks during the day, the line stabilised and
though there was serious fighting for the village between the 11 and 14
November, which put serious strain on the German defenders and drove
them to the verge of breaking point in this area, the front line remained
just to the east and north of the village throughout the remaining weeks
of the Battle of the Somme.

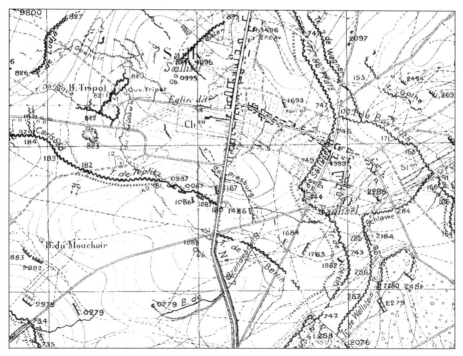

Sailly-Saillisel Trench Map, October 1916.

Le Transloy: the monument and ossuary commemorating the 'Combats of Le Transloy' of 28 August and 26 September 1914.

Once through Sailly-Saillisel, turn right onto the N17 and continue northwards to Le Transloy.

*Turn left onto the D19 in Le Transloy and after 1,200 metres **Le Transloy communal cemetery** (13) is reached.*

A monument, several graves and an ossuary (containing the remains of 792 soldiers) commemorate the '700 Braves' of the 'Combats of Le Transloy' of 28 August and 26 September 1914 that were fought here. During the general retreat of August 1914, the *62e Division d'Infanterie* (a reserve division, consisting of reservists from Haute-Vienne, Charente, Creuse and Vienne) had been moved forward by train from Ivry-sur-Seine via Godesse and Arras to Douai, where they arrived on the 26 August 1914. The following day, they marched south towards Péronne and bivouacked between Haplincourt and Bertincourt, blissfully unaware of the proximity of the German II Corps approaching Péronne and the western River Somme from the north east, and Marwitz's Cavalry Corps that was shadowing them from the direction of Beaumetz les Cambrai. The *62e Division d'Infanterie,* advancing in a south easterly direction to the immediate east of the *61e Division d'infanterie,* was now on a collision course with the Germans.

In the early morning mist of 28 August the move towards Péronne was continued but contact was made with the Germans in the vicinity of Rocquigny, Le Transloy, Côte 123, Morval, Sailly-Saillisel and the approach to Moislains. Heavily outnumbered, the French put up a brave fight but were forced to withdraw – the *62e Division d'Infanterie* retreating northwards towards Arras and the *61e Division d'Infanterie* heading through Flers towards Albert and, ultimately, Amiens. Some elements broke through in a southerly direction through Rancourt and managed to cross the River Somme between Cléry and Hem.

The *263e* and *338e Régiments d'Infanterie* of *123e Brigade, 62e Division d'Infanterie* suffered 1,299 and 1,139 casualties respectively in this action that lasted less than two hours. Out of the nearly 800 soldiers buried in the mass grave at Le Transloy, nearly 700 are from the *338e Régiment d'Infanterie*.

Continue along the D19 to Lesboeufs.

In Lesboeufs, turn left onto the D74, through Morval and on towards Combles.

Immediately before entering Combles, note that there is a **German concrete command post** *(**14**) located in the field to the right.*

Enter Combles and turn left onto the D20.

German Command Post at the entrance to Combles.

Memorial to Sous – Lieutenant Charles Dansette of the *43e Régiment d'infanterie* just before the motorway bridge at Combles.

*Follow the road through Combles for just under a kilometre and, immediately before the motorway bridge, the **Memorial to Sous-Lieutenant Charles Dansette** of the 43e Régiment d'infanterie (**15**) can be seen in front of a sports field on the right.*

Born in Armentières, Nord, on 5 October 1894, Charles Alfred Adrien Dansette was a student prior to his enlistment. He voluntarily enlisted into the *43e Régiment d'infanterie* at Lille on 26 March 1913 and was promoted to *caporal* in November 1913. After seeing action at the Battles of Guise and the Marne in 1914, he was promoted to *sergent* prior to fighting at the Battle of the Aisne. Throughout 1915 and into 1916

Charles fought on the Aisne and Champagne fronts and then Verdun before, via another stint on the Aisne, moving to the Somme in August 1916. Commissioned as a *sous-Lieutenant* on 19 September 1916, Charles was killed in action whilst leading an assault on a German trench forward of Le Priez Ferme and Frégiecourt just six days later, on 25 September 1916.

In 1,100 metres the road passes the location of Charles Dansette's death, **Le Priez Ferme (16)**, *on the left.*

The Third Line fortified redoubt position of Le Priez Farm as it is today. Heavily fought over, it fell to the *46e Division d'infanterie* on 14 September 1916.

A fortified redoubt and strongpoint in the German Third Line of defence, Le Priez Ferme was protected by up to six rows of trenches and belts of barbed wire. It was captured on 14 September 1916 by the *chasseurs* of the *46e Division d'infanterie,* who narrowly failed to secure nearby Frégiecourt (deemed as a necessary start point for the Anglo-French attacks of 15 September). During the 15 September operation a little progress was made towards Rancourt to the north of Le Priez Ferme, but this was stopped dead by artillery and machine gun fire. A German counter-attack in this area on 20/21 September was successfully defeated.

***Rancourt German Cemetery* (17)** *is reached (on the right) after a further 1,500 metres*

Testament to the ferocity of the actions in the area; an unusually large amount of unexploded French F1 handgrenades (plus a couiple of Vivien-Bessier rifle grenades) amongst the more commonly encountered detritus by the side of Le Priez Farm.

The largest of the three cemeteries from different nationalities in the immediate vicinity; Rancourt German Military Cemetery.

Rancourt German Cemetery was created by the French in 1920. It now contains the remains of 11,422 German soldiers (with 7,492 in a *kameradengrab* mass grave) with death dates from throughout the war (though the majority date from July – December 1916). Like most other German cemeteries, this is a concentration cemetery and contains some graves from as far afield as Arras. Unusually for the Somme, the grave markers in this cemetery are stone crosses (with the occasional floor plaque).

*Continue to the N17 and turn left toward the **Nécropole nationale de Rancourt** (18)*

A 'flagship cemetery' for the French, the *Nécropole nationale de Rancourt* contains the remains of 8,566 French soldiers (and three civilians) from 1914-18 and one from 1939-45. 3,240 of these are contained within the four ossuaries. Formed in 1921 from a concentration of the small French cemeteries around Combles, Cléry and Curlu, it continued to expand with the concentration of remains discovered on the battlefields between 1945 and 1973. In 1980 the graves from isolated graves and military sections in communal cemeteries from Flixecourt and Bus-la-Mésière were also concentrated here. The cemetery was listed as 'complete' in 1988.

The French Somme 'flagship' cemetery; the *Nécropole nationale de Rancourt*.

Private memorials within the *Souvenir Français* chapel. A particularly interesting one lists the French units that fought in the Battle of the Somme.

Well worth a vist, adjoining the cemetery is a *Souvenir Français* chapel that contains numerous private memorials (including several to individual British soldiers), a nearby information centre and a small museum.

Across the road can be seen Rancourt British Cemetery **(19)**.

The chapel and cemetery as it appeared in 1921.

RANCOURT-BOUCHAVESNES 1922.
L'Église et un coin du Cimetière - Section 1.

Begun by the Guards Division after the British took over the lines here during the winter of 1916/17, the cemetery was used again in September 1918 by the 12th and 18th Divisions. Six isolated graves from nearby were relocated here after the Armistice. Containing ninety three burials from 1914-18, twenty of these are unidentified (but there is a special memorial to one of these who is known to be amongst the unidentified). Three unknown airmen, who were killed in May 1940, are also buried in this cemetery.

Continue up the N17 and through the eastern edge of Rancourt village **(20)**.

Rancourt was captured on 25 September 1916 by the *42e Division d'infanterie* during another joint Anglo-French cooperation (known to the British as The Battle of Morval). Following a heavy bombardment of the German positions, the French left their trenches in the old German defences around Le Priez Ferme and within minutes finally captured Frégicourt. Also advancing eastwards, Rancourt and its defences were overrun and the advance continued to the north-west corner of Bois Saint Pierre Vaast, where the line would settle for the remainder of the battle.

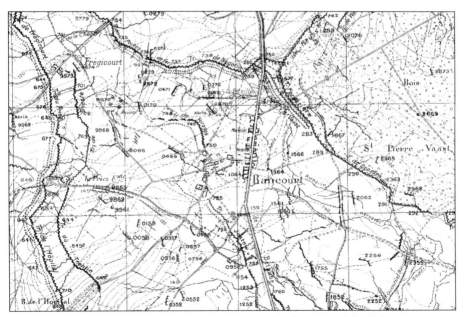

Rancourt Trench Map, dated October 1916, showing part of the defences on the western edge of Bois St Pierre Vaast and marking the limit of the French advance in this area during the Battle of the Somme.

141

The north-western part of the 'unconquerable' Bois St Pierre Vaast, north of Rancourt, illustrating the open ground that had to be traversed in any attempt to storm the massed machine guns and positions hidden in the dense woodland. By September 1916 this field contained no less than three rows of German trenches and was a veritable sea of barbed wire.

Once through the village of Rancourt, take the first small road to the right (before the water tower that you can see on the left). At the end of the track in front of you, where the track reaches the trees of Bois Saint Pierre Vaast, is the limit of the French advance here during the Battle of the Somme and marks the point reached by the 42e Division d'infanterie on 25 September **(21)**.

Remaining in German hands throughout the battle, the Bois Saint Pierre Vaast was assaulted by the French on numerous occasions between September and November 1916, with no less than eleven divisions taking part in the actions here throughout this period. Fortified with thick barbed wire entanglements, an intricate trench system, concrete shelters, a large number of machine gun emplacements and, further back, artillery batteries, even the lie of the land favoured the defender, with the eastern limits being on a height that dominated the French lines and much of the land westwards. The wood appeared and, indeed, proved to be, unconquerable (it was finally taken, unopposed, by the British Army following the German withdrawal of February 1917).

First reached by the *14e Division d'infanterie* on 13/14 September 1916, an unsuccessful attempt to push into the southern section of the wood and Bois Germain followed the capture of Bouchavesnes. A further, failed, attempt was made the following day and the line consolidated. The next major action in front of the southern section of the wood was a

German action that took place on the night of the 19/20 September when, during a large scale counter-attack, an attempt was made to recapture Bouchavesnes.

On 25 September 1916 the *42e Division d'infanterie*, after their successful advance through Rancourt, managed to capture the German trench located slightly forward of the tree line in the north western corner of the wood (*Tranchée de Bois Saint Vaast*) but failed to progress further. The position proving to be untenable, they were forced to withdraw some fifty metres or so to where the new French frontline became established. Further attempts to penetrate into the wood during the general attack of 26 October and on the following day proved just as fruitless.

On 6 October 1916, in support of the first attack on Sailly-Saillisel, an assault was successful in diverting some German attention from the more northerly actions; but, again, the wood remained impenetrable. A final attempt, launched at 11.30am on 5 November 1916 after a terrific French bombardment of the wood, was met by a horrendous retaliatory bombardment on the attacking Frenchmen. In the northwest corner, the *6e, 27e* and *28e Bataillons Alpin de chasseurs à pied* managed to penetrate into the wood itself but, after coming up against undamaged machine gun emplacements and thick tangles of wire located within the ruined trees, they were forced to retire. By 7pm the attack was over and the survivors had returned to their start positions.

Return to the N17.

GPS Waypoints, Tour 1 Part 3

1 - 49°59'9.98"N, 2°52'51.05"E	2 - 49°58'53.48"N, 2°52'25.63"E
3 - 49°57'30.01"N, 2°53'3.20"E	4 - 49°57'6.85"N, 2°53'30.25"E
5 - 49°58'10.22"N, 2°54'14.57"E	6 - 49°58'32.28"N, 2°55'29.27"E
7 - 49°58'38.18"N, 2°55'7.12"E	8 - 49°59'2.18"N, 2°54'55.96"E
9 - 49°59'5.47"N, 2°55'4.26"E	10 - 49°59'3.23"N, 2°55'18.80"E
11 - 50° 0'3.89"N, 2°57'40.33"E	12 - 50° 1'36.51"N, 2°55'14.54"E
13 - 50° 3'16.94"N, 2°52'55.31"E	14 - 50° 0'49.83"N, 2°52'10.49"E
15 - 50° 0'25.17"N, 2°52'29.92"E	16 - 50° 0'10.00"N, 2°53'12.54"E
17 - 49°59'49.59"N, 2°54'19.36"E	18 - 49°59'51.87"N, 2°54'39.40"E
19 - 49°59'53.27"N, 2°54'35.34"E	20 - 50° 0'18.63"N, 2°54'37.48"E
21 - 50° 0'30.95"N, 2°54'45.95"E	

End of Tour 1

Tour 2: South of the Somme
Part 1 – 1 July

START: Crossroads at the centre of **Foucaucourt en Santerre (1)**

A front line village on the main Amiens to St Quentin Roman road (now the N29), the road marked the demarcation line between the *219e Régiment d'infanterie* and the *262e Régiment d'infanterie* (both of the *61e Division d'infanterie*) on 1 July 1916. On this date, the French front lay 800 metres east of the centre of the village – approximately midway between your present location and the expanse of woodland that you can see on either side of the road in the direction of St Quentin.

At 9.30am on 1 July 1916, following the bombardment of the German front lines and rear – including hitting the first day objective of Bois du Satyre with over 40,000 gas shells – the *262e Régiment d'infanterie* (the southernmost regiment of all the attacking units on this first day) went over the top and attacked in a roughly north easterly direction, gradually crossing the Roman road as they moved towards Bois de Satyre (the woodland north of the road) in conjunction with the *219e Régiment d'infanterie* to their immediate north . Reaching and attaining the first objective (the western fringe of the wood) within ten minutes of the launch of the assault, the *262e* had to remain conscious of the need to retain some troops on the south of the road to protect the exposed flank of the attack as they advanced through the German lines (this was also protected to the south of Foucaucourt by the *51e Division d'infanterie* who, other than supplying fire support, played no part in the 1 July advance).

On the N29 through Foucaucourt, travel eastwards for 1.8 kilometres until the woodland (2) is reached.

Between the end of 1 July 1916 and 4 July, the road through this woodland marked the southern front line with the French holding the north of the road and the Germans holding the south (note the number of craters, trenches and other scarring still visible within the trees on either side of the road). On 4 July the front here was pushed slightly southwards into the wood some 150 metres away from the road.

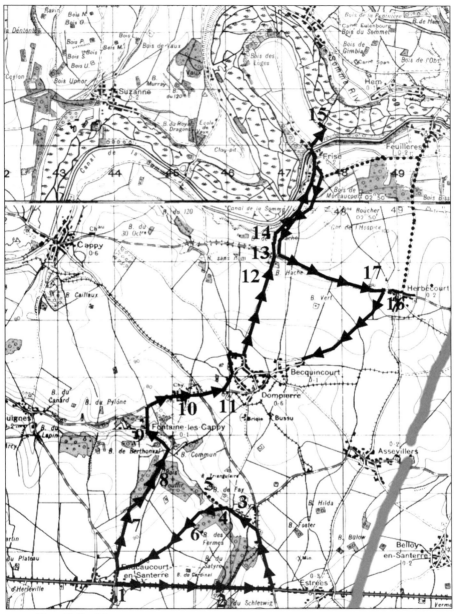

Tour 2, Part 1.

Bois du Satyre

Bois de Soyecourt

The Amiens – St Quentin road dividing Bois du Satyre (left) and Bois de Soyécourt (right).

*To the north of the road the woodland is called the **Bois du Satyre** and to the south it is **Bois de Soyécourt**.*

Once the western edge of Bois du Satyre had been reached, reconnaissance patrols were sent into the wood for the next couple of hours until, at 12.50pm, the advance continued. Progress was made with some difficulty through the fallen trees and was occasionally held up by German machine gun fire. German heavy artillery began to bombard the wood. However, by the late afternoon of 1 July, all of the objectives had been taken and the *262e* and *219 e Régiments d'infanterie* were consolidating their newly won positions on the eastern fringe of the wood.

*Continue for a further 950 metres and, at the crossroads just before the village of Estrées- Deniècourt, turn left onto the D164. At the next crossroads, upon which **Fay village cemetery** is located, turn left towards the (current) church of the village of Fay **(3)**. On the wall here can be seen some **memorial plaques** dedicated to **Capitaine Félix Paul Fontan** of the 99e Régiment d'infanterie, who was mortally wounded at Fay on 18 December 1914, and **Sous-Lieutenant Ernest Champin** of the 329e Régiment d'infanterie, who was killed near Fay on 4 July 1916. Another plaque commemorates the actions of the 10e compagnie of the 41e Régiment d'infanterie at Fay on 7 June 1940.*

Félix Paul Émile Fontan was born at Aignan, Gers, on 30 October 1880. In October 1900 he entered the Military School at St Cyr and graduated as a *sous-lieutenant* in the *157e Régiment d'infanterie* in October 1902. Awarded the *Médaille d'honneur pour acte de courage et de dévouement* in bronze for his rescue efforts during an avalanche at the Col de la Pare in the Alps in February 1904, Félix (known as Paul) was also promoted to *lieutenant*. He transferred to the gendarmerie as a *lieutenant* in July 1908 and was appointed to the *légion de la garde rèpublicaine* in Paris in 1912. A second *Médaille d'honneur pour acte de courage et de dévouement*, this time in gold, was awarded in May 1912 for his role in the apprehension and destruction of the anarchist and criminal Bonnot Gang at Choissy-le-Roi the previous month. Soon after the outbreak of war Paul applied for a voluntary transfer to an infantry unit and, on 16 October 1914, was transferred as a *lieutenant* to the *99e Régiment d'infanterie*. Promoted to (temporary) *capitaine* on 25 October 1914, he joined his new regiment while they were holding the line between Dompierre and Fay. After the *99e Régiment d'infanterie* was heavily engaged in a vicious small scale action at Fay on 10 December 1914, the next week was spent in harassing raids and reconnaissance. During the preparation for one of these raids, on 18 December 1914, Paul was shot in the head and grievously injured. He died the following day in *Ambulance Nr.2* at Villers-Bretonneux.

Plaques to *Capitaine* Félix Paul Fontan, *Sous-Lieutenant* Ernest Champin and the *10e compagnie* of the *41e Régiment d'infanterie* (1940) on the wall of the village church at Fay.

Ernest Léon Champin was the parish priest from Ste Désir in Lisieux, Normandy, at the time of the outbreak of war. He was born at Berjou, Orne, on 15 February 1884 and had been ordained in June 1909, becoming curate at Isigny before being transferred to Lisieux in 1911. *L'abbé* Champin had had his compulsory military service before the war deferred due to his occupation and was enlisted into the *service auxiliaire* instead. On 15 March 1915 he was transferred into the military, serving as a *soldat 2e classe* in the *5e Régiment d'Infanterie;* but he was soon earmarked for officer training and appointed *aspirant* on 20 August 1915. Transferred to the *74e Régiment d'Infanterie* on 23 August 1915, he then moved to the *329e Régiment d'Infanterie* on 28 August for active service. After taking part in the fighting in the Tahure sector during the Second Battle of Champagne in September and October 1915, Ernest was commissioned as a *sous-lieutenant* on 10 October 1915 and moved to the Somme the following year. Not involved in the opening day of the Battle of the Somme, the *329e Régiment d'Infanterie* took part in the attack on the northern part of Estrées on evening of the 4 July 1916. Attacking at 5.30pm from trenches near *Bois Foster* (about a kilometre east of Fay), Estrées was successfully entered and was largely in French hands by 9pm. However, a large German counter-attack took place at around this time and, whilst attempting to give aid to a wounded soldier, Ernest was shot through the head. Initially buried in the cemetery at Fay, he is now interred in the nécropole nationale de Dompierre-Becquincourt, but presently appears to be missing from the online Sépultures de Guerre database.

Beyond the church, take the left fork and follow the road round to the **ruins of the old village of Fay (4)**.

No stranger to war, the village of Fay has had to be rebuilt twice (once partially) during the past 150 years. The centre of the current incarnation, though parts are built over the remains of the old village, was relocated to a point a couple of hundred meters east of the old and nearer to the D164 road. It had a population of 153 in 1913.

Severely damaged during skirmishes between General Edwin von Manteuffel's VIII Corps and Général Louis Faidherbe's *Armée du Nord* in December 1870 following the Battles of Amiens (16 December) and Pont Noyelles (23 December), it was the scene of a small action between *franc tireurs* and a patrol from the 8th Uhlans on 11 December 1870 in which two Uhlans were killed (they were buried in Estrées cemetery). Fay was also hit by German artillery as a precautionary measure during the siege of Péronne on 6 January 1871. The damaged buildings were repaired or rebuilt in their original locations.

Preserved remains of the old village of Fay.

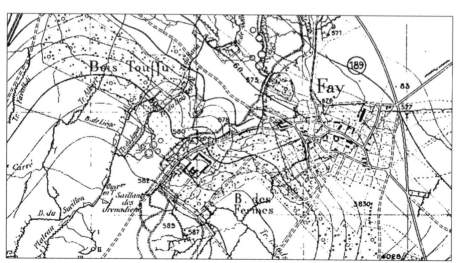

Fay Trench Map, April 1916.

On 29 August 1914 the German army once again arrived at Fay as the First Army advanced on Paris. Returning within a month, they began to dig in and, in October 1914, started to establish the village as a fortified front line position. Three times in the following two months the French attempted to take the village, but with disastrous results and so an underground war began. From the first detonation in April 1915 through to January 1916, mine warfare ensued to the immediate north and, to a lesser extent, the east of the village; yet the line still seemed immovable.

On 1 July 1916 the task of the capture of this village fell to the *264e* and *265e Régiments d'infanterie* of the *61e Division d'infanterie*. Following on from the five days of continuous bombardment on the village and defences, the *264e and 265e Régiments d'infanterie* launched their assault at 9.30am. Meeting very little opposition to the south of the village, the *264e* secured its objectives of the farm, wood and cemetery of Fay with ease. They then moved along *Tranchée de Lützow* to take Bois Foster and to keep parallel with the *265e Régiment*'s advance.

To their immediate north, the *265e* moved through the ruins of the village itself, clearing the cellars and shelters of their shell-shocked occupants as they progressed. Troubled by just a single machine gun as they advanced, the first objective, the Cappy – Estrées road, was taken within the first hours and, during the afternoon, the second objective, *Tranchée de Loge,* running vertically from Bois Foster, was also attained. Originally scheduled to take a third objective, the strong defensive line between Bois de Glatz and Bois Bülow south of Assevillers and to the west of Belloy, it was, sensibly, decided to call a halt to the advance here for the day to avoid forming a salient into German held territory that would be difficult to defend.

During this first day the *265e Régiment d'infanterie* lost thirty seven killed and 198 wounded. The figures for the *264e* are unavailable.

The excavated ruins of the old village of Fay that you can see are only a small portion of the original village near to and including the old church of St Martin. The front line lay to the north-west and west of this location.

Return back to the main road and turn left (in a westward direction, noting that a section of this road is named in memory of Capitaine Fontan). After 200 metres, there is a T junction (at the Place du Capitaine Fontan). Though the rather narrow route continues straight on (beyond an access only no-entry sign) towards Foucaucourt at this junction (following part of the 1916 German front line), it is an interesting detour to turn right and travel up the single file track towards Fontaine les Cappy for about 150 metres. At this point (5) stop and look to the right.

Remains of the church of St Martin, Fay, in August 1916.

The old St Martin's church today.

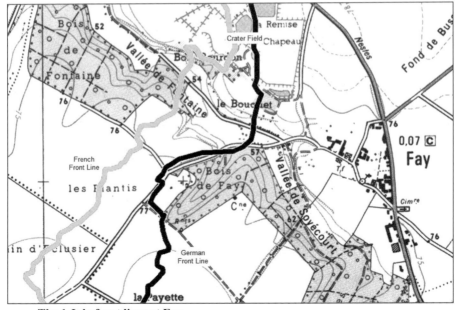

The 1 July front lines at Fay.

The German front line was just to the right of your field of vision with that of the French to the left, crossing the road you are on at the point where the woodland (Bois Touffu) on the left begins and continuing to and around the small woodland (the 'Bois de Fay' as it was in 1916) on the right of the road.

In 1916, this area was a crater field and was evidence of the intense mine warfare in the area during 1915. By August 1915 eighteen mine craters of varying size (six French and twelve German) scarred this ground. As an indication of the intensity of operations, no less than eighty eight camouflets (small charge defensive mines) had also been detonated in the same area.

7. - FAY (Somme). — Un trou de Mine de 39 mètres de profondeur.
A Mine-hole of 39 m. depth.

One of the larger mine craters to be found in the Fay crater fields – evidence of the intensive underground war conducted in the area throughout 1915.

Looking back to the French front line (from where the corner of Bois Touffu meets the road in front of you, and skirting Bois de Fay on the opposite side of the road before heading due north), you are looking at the southernmost area from which the *7e Régiment d'infanterie coloniale* of the *3e Division d'infanterie coloniale* attacked on 1 July 1916 (Bois de Fay being the boundary between the *61e Division d'infanterie* and the *3e Division d'infanterie coloniale*).

Attacking eastwards (from left to right as you look at it from your current position), from Bois de Fay northwards, the *7e Régiment d'infanterie coloniale* were tasked with the capture of Bois Triangulaire, the crossroads north of Fay and the southern slopes of the Bussu rise, along with the five lines of German trenches in between. If possible, they were to push on as far as Bois des Loges and the beetroot factory in front of Assevillers. Following the intense bombardment that lasted until 9.30am on 1 July 1916, they came under a German counter bombardment and so pushed on quickly into and through the German first line, securing it, and capturing Bois Triangulaire by 10am. By midday they had moved on beyond the Fay crossroads and were holding the Bussu rise; but they had lost contact with the *265e Régiment d'infanterie* on their right due to the speed of their assault. After digging in and waiting to regain contact with the *265e,* an order was received to push on as their current position was too exposed. By 4pm contact had been re-established and at 6pm, after capturing Bois des Loges and the beetroot factory on the crossroads west of Assevillers, the advance stopped and consolidation began. At 9pm a battalion sized German counter-attack managed to penetrate into the French positions, but was eventually beaten back.

The following few days showed slow progression in this area as they steadily moved forward through Assevillers before being relieved by the *Régiment de marche de la Légion étrangère* on 4 July.

Losses for the regiment between 1 and 4 July amounted to 104 killed and 528 wounded and missing.

Return to the junction (there is an area where it is possible to turn a car around at the western point of Touffu Wood) and turn right towards Foucaucourt, noting that this is also an extremely narrow single track road and is not suitable for larger vehicles. Continue for a further 720 metres until the trees thin out on the left **(6)**. *This is the site of the farm, fortified by the Germans, that gave the name to the wood* **(Bois des Fermes)** *that you have just driven through.*

[For an alternative route to this point of the tour, return via Fay to the N29 and turn right towards Foucaucourt. Just beyond Bois de Satyre, take the first right and continue for just under 400 metres. Turn left for another 700 metres before turning right (in the heart of the No Man's Land of 1 July). After 650 metres, the next point is reached.]

The perimeter of Bois de Fermes follows the German front line of 1 July. The wood and farm were captured by the *265e Régiment d'infanterie* during the first hour of the battle. Like so many of the front line woods on the Somme, this wood still contains traces of the shell holes and trenches from this period. Ruined remains of some of the farm buildings are also still visible within the trees.

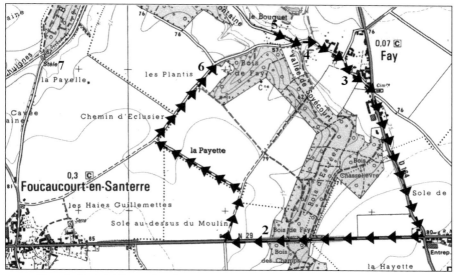

Tour 2, Part 1 Alternative detour.

Scene inside Bois des Fermes following its capture on 1 July. Numerous, rather extravagant, dugouts existed within the trees.

The Bois des Fermes. Area of the German front line and location of the farm that gave the name to the woodland.

From here, with your back to the clearing, a good view can be had of the French line, parallel with the road some seventy five metres into the field at your front and pulling back to the boundary of Bois Touffu to your right front, and the No Man's Land crossed on 1 July. The small road you can see running towards Bois Touffu marks the regimental boundary for 1 July. To the right of it, in the direction of Fay, was the attack line of the *265e Régiment d'infanterie* and, to the left, that of the *264e*. Recently, a small information panel has been erected at this spot.

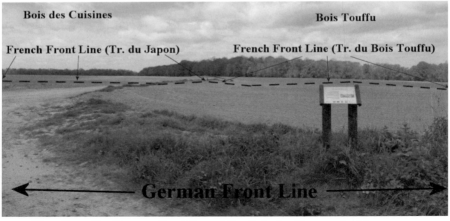

View from the German front line at the Bois des Fermes, looking across towards the French lines in front of Bois Touffu. Another crater field, in the middle distance (to the left of the track), was a cluster of five medium sized mine craters by the end of 1915. This was the battlefield of the *265e Régiment d'infanterie* on 1 July.

*Continue on this road towards Foucaucourt. Take the first right turn and then, almost immediately the right fork. After 900 metres, a small **1915** **memorial** (7) can be encountered on the left verge just before the wood. Unfortunately, the inscription on this memorial is now illegible. Continue up this road, with the Bois de Cuisines on your left, for one kilometre. On your left is a pair of memorials to the 205e Régiment d'infanterie and the 1e Régiment du Génie* **(8)**.

One memorial commemorates the actions of the ***205e Régiment d'infanterie*** in their disastrous attack on Fay on 30 November 1914, where they were cut up by machine gun fire after being caught on thick belts of barbed wire in front of Bois des Fermes, and their actions on the Somme as from 3 July 1916 in the Foucaucourt and Estrées areas. The other memorial commemorates the engineers of the ***5/7e*** and ***5/7e bis compagnies*** attached to the ***1e Régiment du Génie*** and their operations in this area through 1914 and 1915.

The *205e Régiment d'infanterie* and *1e Régiment du Génie* 1914/15 memorials in between Bois de Cuisines and Bois Touffu.

Upon reaching the crossroads, turn left towards Fontaine les Cappy **(9)** *where a visit here can be made to the French war grave in the churchyard and next to which is the site of a small British cemetery that was relocated post-war.*

Among the British casualties who were buried here were three tunnellers killed during the brief interlude when British divisions held the line here during the autumn of 1915. Their remains were concentrated to Hangard Communal Cemetery after the war.

Take the first right in Fontaine les Cappy onto the D71E. As you travel up this short stretch of road, look to your right. 850 metres distant is the location of the French front line from where the 58e Régiment d'infanterie coloniale launched their attack on 1 July.

The 58e Régiment d'infanterie coloniale attacked across the open ground to the south of Dompierre on 1 July 1916. Breaking through five lines of German trenches, they managed to storm the high-ground strongpoint of Ferme Bussu and take the woods and observation point at 'Point 557-b' whilst keeping pace with their fast moving neighbours (the *7e Régiment d'infanterie coloniale*) to the south. After capturing *Tranchées de Glatz* and *Retz* at bayonet point, the day ended with the regiment located just outside the north west corner of Asseviller. On 2 and 3 July they moved the line forward and then took part in the capture of Asseviller.

By the time the *58e Régiment d'infanterie coloniale* was relieved, they had lost ninety one dead, 562 wounded and 120 missing.

*At the junction, turn right onto the D71 towards Dompierre-Becquincourt. After 700 metres, on land now occupied by a (now defunct) post war sugar factory, is the site of the original **Dompierre Sucrerie (10)**.*

The sucrerie of Dompierre as it appeared in 1916.

The site of Dompierre sucrerie today.

Being one of the largest buildings and one of the most famous landmarks in this sector, the Dompierre Sucrerie had existed here since 1879. From October 1914 it was located a mere 300 meters behind the French front line but, due to its sheer scale and the thickness of its walls, it gave a welcome respite and shelter to thousands of French soldiers who served in this sector, even though it was a regular target for the German guns. Mentioned in many diaries from the war, it had many roles, serving as a company headquarters, aid station, barracks, observation post or just simply a shelter. Nearly totally destroyed during the war, rebuilding began in 1922.

*Continue straight across the crossroads until the **Nécropole nationale de Dompierre-Becquincourt** (11) is reached on your right. Note the communal cemetery next to the military cemetery. The German front line of 1 July 1916 actually ran through this civilian cemetery.*

Built immediately behind the 1 July German front line – the Nécropole nationale de Dompierre-Becquincourt.

159

Created in 1920, the *Nécropole nationale* now contains the remains of 7,032 French soldiers from the First World War and one German. There is also the grave of a French soldier from the Second World War. 1,671 of these soldiers lie in the four ossuaries. Extended in 1935 and 1936 with the concentration of small cemeteries from various locations on the Somme battlefields, many isolated graves were also moved here between 1948 and 1985. A monument was erected in the cemetery, funded by the Italian residents of Dompierre in memory of their 'French comrades who died for France'. Extensive views of the battlefields to the south and west can be had from the rear of this cemetery.

*A visit to the village of **Dompierre** can be made from here.*

The war first came near to Dompierre on 26 August 1914 when distant gunfire prompted the inhabitants of Dompierre and Becquincourt to flee. The next day a German plane flew low over the village and, after a farm in Becquincourt was set alight, Uhlan patrols entered and occupied the villages.

The return of the French army on 14 September 1914 following the Battle of the Marne tempted some of the population to return; but the villages came under intensive shell fire for five days from 26 September as the Germans moved back towards them. Between the 30 and 31 October hand to hand fighting between French and German troops took place in and around the village and the French were pushed back beyond the western outskirts of Dompierre, where they dug in and formed a trench system. With the Germans digging in opposite, Dompierre then became a German front line village (the remaining inhabitants were evacuated by them on 9 November 1914) until the Battle of the Somme in 1916, with the west and north west of Dompierre becoming another underground battleground in the tunnelers' war between March and July 1915. The crater field thus created was very extensive, underlining the importance of the high ground on which the village stood.

On 1 July 1916 Dompierre-Becquincourt was an objective for the *21e* (southern section of the village) and *23e Régiments d'infanterie coloniale* (to the north).

Occupying the sector in front of the sucrerie, the *21e Régiment d'infanterie coloniale* moved into the trenches at 5am on 1 July and between 7 and 7.30am waited as the artillery, which had been pounding the lines around Dompierre remorselessly for five days, simulated an impending attack. Just before 9.30am, several small mines were detonated under the German positions in front of Dompierre and the infantry assault was launched. After simply walking over No Man's Land, the remains of the German forward trenches and capturing the area of the cemetery and

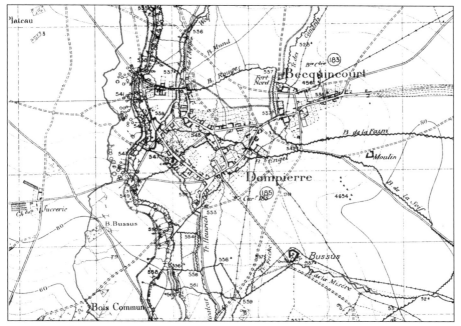

Dompierre Trench Map, June 1916.

Bois Bussu, *Tranchée Heinrich* (the main German trench on the outskirts of the actual buildings of the village) was reached and occupied within fifteen minutes of the start.

Pushing on through the village, Becquincourt was entered and Bussus Mill captured with very little loss. By this point 400 prisoners and six machine guns had been taken and the reserve battalions remained at the start point. However, during the afternoon, orders were received to push on to take the German Second Line position, the *Tranchée de Brunehilde.* This involved moving across very open, slightly raised land, making the infantry very easy targets for the massed machine guns located in Asseviliers. At 3.45pm, following an artillery preparation, the advance was resumed, with bombers fighting down the *boyeau de la Faim* to provide a route across the plateau that was less exposed to Asseviliers. Sections of the *Tranchée de Brunehilde* were taken and held by evening. (*Brunehilde* was held for the next two days, with small scale but violent actions continuing as further sections were taken and several counter-attacks fought off. Asseviliers was then captured before the regiment was relieved. During the period 1 – 4 July, the *21e Régiment d'infanterie coloniale* lost fourteen officers and 472 other ranks, with most of these casualties incurred between Becquincourt and Asseviliers.

Zouaves inspecting graves in the (remarkably intact) German military cemetery at Becquincourt in the days following the capture of Dompierre – Becquincourt.

To their north, opposite the northern part of Dompierre, the *23e Régiment d'infanterie coloniale* had been tasked with a similar role – the capture of Dompierre, Becquincourt and an advance to the German Second Line positions between Herebecourt and Assevillers, approximately two and a half kilometres distant. Preceding the attack by numerous patrols to gauge the extent of the destruction caused by the artillery preparation, the regimental advance at 9.30am followed after the firing of the mines. As with the *21e Régiment's* attack, the advance through Dompierre was relatively unopposed and, following the capture of Becquincourt, the advance paused while the artillery bombarded the German Second Line and its approaches. At 3.45pm, in conjunction with its sister regiment to the south, the *23e* attacked the German Second Line. Though under heavy fire, all objectives were seized by 7pm.

Return westwards down the road you have just travelled for 150 metres (from the French cemetery entrance) and turn sharp right and then left at the crossroads, which marks the dividing line between the 21e and 23e Régiments d'infanterie coloniale. This road follows the German front of July 1916, which was in the fields eighty metres to your left, following the curve of the road. This particular field was another crater field from the mine warfare of 1915 and was the location of the small mines detonated prior to the attack on the morning of 1 July.

162

Turn right once the limit of the village has been reached and then left onto the D471. For 1,300 metres this road follows the pre-January 1916 German front line. This was advanced westwards by some 500 metres during the 'combats de Frise' between 28 January and 14 February 1916. In 1.8 kilometres (from joining the D471 at Dompierre), just before the crossroads, the pre-1916 French front line position of **Bois Hache (12)** *is reached – the southernmost extent of which led into another small crater field dating from 1915.*

600 metres to the left of the length of road you have just travelled was the jumping off points of (south to north) the *8e, 4e and 24e Régiments d'infanterie coloniale* on 1 July, who all managed to advance through seven lines of trenches and thick barbed wire to reach the open Herbécourt Plateau and come within grenade distance of *Fortin Kronprinz* by the evening of the first day - an advance of 1,700 metres and a testimony to effective artillery preparation. However, they were ordered to withdraw slightly to more defendable positions after repeated attempts to break into the village of Herbécourt failed.

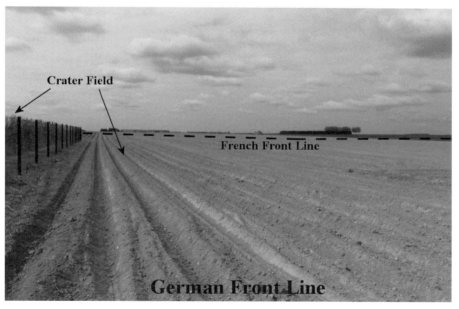

Looking towards the French lines from the German 1 July front at the northern entry to Dompierre (over the land captured by *23e Régiment d'infanterie coloniale* **on the first day). The Dompierre crater field was to the immediate front and to the left (beyond the fence) of this photograph.**

The crossroads near Bois Hache (the pre-January 1916 French front line), looking in the direction of the 1 July attack by the *22e Régiment d'infanterie coloniale*

At the crossroads **(13)** *you are in the centre of the area through which the 22e Régiment d'infanterie coloniale attacked on 1 July.*

Attacking down and either side of the road (now the D1) running left to right across your front, the *22e Régiment d'infanterie coloniale* start point was 600 metres to the west of your present location, with three lines of trenches in between. This crossroads sits exactly on the third row of trenches which, prior to January 1916, was the French second position. To your right lay another four rows of trenches, the last three of which were the pre-January 1916 German forward and front lines and were formidable obstacles, with thick belts of wire and a myriad of shelters and emplacements.

The *22e Régiment d'infanterie coloniale* launched their assault at 9.30am and managed to advance comfortably across the destroyed German lines until about 1.30pm, when they came under cross fire from the north and from Herbécourt whilst crossing the open areas of the Plaine de Becquincourt. Ordered to dig in, it became apparent that the *36e Régiment d'infanterie coloniale* to their north was struggling to achieve their objectives. The *22e* lost sixty one men killed on 1 July.

*Continue over the crossroads and, as you drive towards the river, note that the field to your right contained the French pre-1916 front line and was yet another crater field, and a consequence of the 1915 mine warfare in the region. Before the road swings to the right, turn left and follow a rather inadequate road to visit the **Bois de la Vache, Belvedere de Frise, quarries, trenches and viewpoint** (14), an area in which, both in the open and (especially) in the wooded areas, it is still possible to discern the original trench lines and see shell holes, etc.*

A viewpoint and nature reserve offering some stunning views over the River Somme and its marshes (including decent views of some of the British battlefields north of the river where, on a good day, it is possible to discern such locations as Leuze Wood, Delville Wood and High Wood, etc.), the Bois de la Vache became a French front line position following the *combats de Frise*. Prior to this event, it was about a kilometre behind the French front and it and its quarries served as headquarters, dressing stations and rest areas, etc. Held by the *36e Régiment d'infanterie coloniale* on 1 July, the objectives of this regiment on the first day was to advance eastwards and north-east along the canal, advancing half way into Frise itself and capturing Garenne Carpezat, Garenne Boucher, Bois Bosquet and to secure the northern part of the Frise-Herbécourt Road. If possible, they were to push on into Bois de Méreaucourt to a point just before Feuilléres.

The area of the Belvédère of Frise attacked by the *36e Régiment d'infanterie coloniale* on 1 July. An area of beauty that affords stunning views, traces of trenches and shell holes can still be encountered reminding the visitor that, in July 1916, this was a German front line position.

A view of the village of Frise prior to the war.

However, this would become one of the two locations where the French did not manage to attain their first day objectives completely. Joining the general assault at 9.30am and quickly moving over the German forward trenches, it soon became apparent that the artillery had not been as effective in the rear of this area as elsewhere. Held up by rifle and machine gun fire from the old, pre January, but still fortified, German First Line, the *36e Régiment d'infanterie coloniale* managed to break through, however, and continued the advance. Sweeping northwards along the canal towards Frise, they came under fire from the massed German machine guns located in the Grenouillére position that had, for over a year now, been a dominant location over the immediate vicinity both north and south of the river. Managing to fight into the cemetery of Frise and to capture the little cluster of woods (Garenne Carpezat, Garenne Boucher, Bois Bosquet and Garenne de l'Hospice) before the Frise-Herbécourt Road, they failed to move into the village itself and secure the road. These objectives, along with Bois de Méreaucourt, would be attained the following day.

Return to the D471, turn left and travel into **Frise**, *noting the village cemetery at the southernmost extreme. This is as far as the 36e Régiment d'infanterie coloniale got into the village on 1 July. Inside the village cemetery is the grave of* **Major George Edmund Borlase Watson, DSO, MC** , *the CO of 'O'Battery, Royal Horse Artillery, who died on 29 August 1918.*

A first day objective for the *36e Régiment d'infanterie coloniale*, the village was captured on 2 July 1916.

Made famous by Blaise Cendrars' book *La Main coupée,* which chronicles his time here with the *3e Régiment de marche du 1er Régiment étrangère* in early 1915, Frise became a front line village on 21 October 1914, with the initial defences being established by troops from the *28e Division d'infanterie,* who were in occupation here until early 1915. Another area (to the south of the village) in which mine warfare was rife throughout 1915, the British Army (14 Brigade, 5th Division) held the line here for a few months from 3 August 1915. On 28 January 1916, the German *11 Infanterie Division* launched an attack on the French *5e Division d'infanterie* here, pushing the line back to within a kilometre of the *9e Brigade* headquarters and putting the Maricourt area north of the river at risk. French artillery, supported by the British artillery north of the river, began a huge bombardment on the German positions and a French counter-attack regained much of the lost territory in the first week of February. Frise would remain in German hands, however, until the Battle of the Somme.

A street in Frise is named after Blaise Cendrars.

A street named after one of the more notable personalities who saw service at Frise.

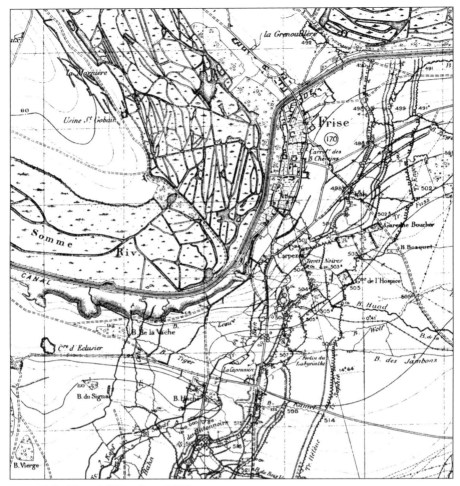

Frise Trench Map, June 1916.

*Remaining on this road, cross over the canal and take an immediate right turn. Following this road takes you to the infamous **La Grenouillére** position* (**15**).

A fortified, heavily entrenched and barricaded machine gun and observation position, this formidable location was a constant thorn in the side for the French (and British) in occupation of Frise and the area around. In control of one of the Somme crossing points, it could cause a nuisance on either side of the river and was a particularly difficult position to access or shell. Mentioned several times by Blaise Cendrars, it was an

168

active location that could hit anywhere within range in Frise or the French canal line. Though it was rendered slightly less effective after the German capture of Frise, it played an important role again on 1 July 1916 in assisting to prevent the advance of the *36e Régiment d'infanterie coloniale* and contributing to their failure to secure all of their objectives on the first day of the Battle of the Somme. At risk from being isolated, the position was abandoned on the evening of the 2 July 1916. The site is now occupied by a camp-site and there are good views of the Somme River from the car park, where it is possible to discern such locations as Monacu Farm on the northern river bank.

The view across the Somme towards Hem from La Grenouillére.

Retrace your route through Frise to the D471. At the five way junction after leaving Frise, 500 metres up the second road from the left (no entry), the road skirts the eastern edge of what was **Garenne Boucher** *(visible on the horizon) which marks the limit of the furthest advance of the 36e Régiment d'infanterie coloniale on 1 July 1916. Continue back up the D471 (direction Dompierre) and turn left on the main road towards* **Herbécourt.**

[Alternatively, take the first road on the left (D471) which goes past **Bois de Méreaucourt,** *captured by the 36e Régiment d'infanterie coloniale on 2 July, with a left turn after the wood on to the D146 going into* **Feuilléres.***]*

A haven behind the German lines from October 1914 to June 1916, Feuilléres served as a headquarters, rest and forward hospital area until it was heavily shelled during the preliminary bombardment for the Battle of the Somme and badly damaged. Almost totally destroyed during the battle, the ruins of the village were captured by the *36e Régiment d'infanterie coloniale* on 3 July 1916. It was from here that, on 30 July, the *2e Régiment mixte de zouaves et tirailleurs* crossed the river to assist in the attack on Monacu Ferme.

Once this visit has been made, return via the D146 to **Herbécourt**

Though **Herbécourt** proved a step too far for the regiments of the *2e Division d'infanterie coloniale* on 1 July, it was taken in its entirety following a swift but heavy artillery barrage during the afternoon of 2 July. Moving in conjunction with the *36e Régiment d'infanterie coloniale* on their left and the *24e Régiment d'infanterie coloniale* on their right, the line was straightened up to the River Somme as the *22e Régiment d'infanterie coloniale* pushed into and took Herbécourt. Moving through the village and setting up a defensive perimeter on the eastern side, a small but easily defendable salient was formed, with wide open views across to the German positions and the German held village of Flaucourt. It was across this open ground, however, that the French would have to advance next.

Once **Herbécourt** *has been reached, turn right onto the D1, noting the large memorial* **(16)** *on the left on the green in front of the church.*

Commemorating the *108e Régiment d'artillerie lourde* and specifically *Aspirant d'artillerie* **Pierre Maistrasse**, who was killed in Herbécourt during a violent counter-battery bombardment on 29 July 1916, the memorial also records the names of several other fallen soldiers along with a quote from General Order No.461 from the 3rd Colonial Corps referring to *Aspirant* Maistrasse. Originally located on or near to the spot at which Pierre was killed (on the road towards Biaches, east of Herbécourt), this memorial was moved to its present location in 1964 to prevent its destruction during the construction of the A1 autoroute.

Memorial at Herbécourt commemorating *Aspirant d'artillerie* **Pierre Maistrasse and his unit, the** *108e Régiment d'artillerie lourde.*

Born in Paris on 26 March 1896, Pierre Alexandre Louis Lucien Maistrasse enlisted in August 1915. After training, he departed for the front at the end of June 1916 and had only been there for a matter of weeks when he was killed in action. Originally buried in the cemetery at Froissy près Chuignolles, his remains were returned home to Paris for burial after the war.

Continue some 200 metres along this road until **Herbécourt British Cemetery** **(17)** *can be seen, situated in a field on the right.*

Aspirant d'artillerie **Pierre Maistrasse.**

Located on the site of the *Fortin Kronprinz* which was reached by the *22e* and *24e Régiments d'infanterie coloniale* on 1 July 1916, but not captured until the 2nd, Herbécourt British Cemetery was started in February 1917. Originally, this cemetery was an extension of the communal cemetery extension that contained the remains of French and German soldiers. The removal of the French and German remains post war left the British cemetery separate from the communal cemetery by some distance and gave it its individual existence. Containing the remains of fifty nine British and Dominion casualties from 1917-18, the cemetery was completed in September 1918.

Return towards Herbécourt (it is possible to turn round after a further 500 metres) and at about 150 metres beyond the cemetery, turn right onto the D71 towards **Becquincourt**.

Immediately to the rear of (and, almost, part of) Dompierre, Beccquincourt was captured as part of the Dompierre operation by the *21e* and *23e Régiments d'infanterie coloniale* on the morning of 1 July 1916.

GPS Waypoints, Tour 2 Part 1

1 - 49°52′28.11″N, 2°46′33.41″E   2 - 49°52′28.77″N, 2°48′3.05″E
3 - 49°53′8.23″N, 2°48′27.12″E   4 - 49°53′12.62″N, 2°48′14.38″E
5 - 49°53′16.35″N, 2°48′3.01″E   6 - 49°53′9.63″N, 2°47′40.46″E
7 - 49°53′10.52″N, 2°46′43.24″E   8 - 49°53′37.74″N, 2°47′6.69″E
9 - 49°53′52.38″N, 2°46′44.98″E   10 - 49°54′14.22″N, 2°47′25.51″E
11 - 49°54′18.99″N, 2°48′4.29″E   12 - 49°55′32.63″N, 2°48′37.13″E
13 - 49°55′36.33″N, 2°48′38.75″E   14 - 49°55′48.62″N, 2°48′23.16″E
15 - 49°56′50.46″N, 2°49′13.26″E   16 - 49°55′19.34″N, 2°50′27.92″E
17 - 49°55′24.23″N, 2°50′7.96″E

Tour 2: South of the Somme
Part 2 – The continuing battle
July – November

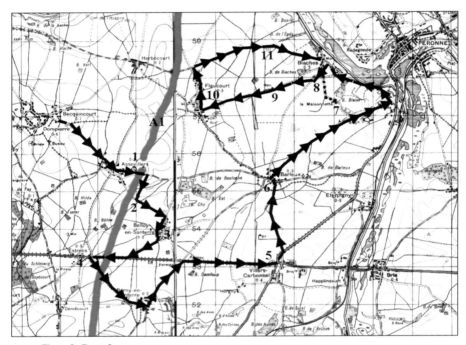

Tour 2, Part 2.

*In Becquincourt take the first road to the left as the village is entered and then left again at the water tower, passing the village cemetery on the right. Continue down this road to **Assevillers**.*

A heavily defended village, protected to the west and north by the formidable *Tranchée de Glatz* and the *Tranchée de Brunehilde*, its capture was imperative to ease the progress of the advance across the Flaucourt Plateau. Parts of *Brunehilde* had been taken on 1 July 1916 and the following day. The French had captured a sufficient length of it until there was just a short distance of open ground to traverse in the inevitable

Assevillers churchyard, July 1916.

assault on the village. Following a preparatory bombardment on 3 July, Assevillers was attacked from the north by the *21e Régiment d'infanterie coloniale* and from the west and south west by the *58e* and *7e Régiments d'infanterie coloniale,* in conjunction with an attack on Flaucourt to the north. By evening the village was firmly in French hands, with the line running between Bois de Vincennes and Bois de Glatz some 500 metres east of the village.

Turn left onto the D4164 and through the centre of the village. Stay on the main road by taking the left road at the Y junction and, just before the bridge over the TGV railway line and motorway, **Assevillers New British cemetery** (1) *can be visited.*

Made after the Armistice by the concentration of several smaller British cemeteries and the transfer of British graves from some French and German cemeteries, Assevillers New British cemetery contains the remains of 482 identified casualties, including those of Olympic gold medal swimmer (Stockholm 1912) Second Lieutenant Cecil Healy, 19th Bn AIF and Second Lieutenant OC Stokes, Royal Munster Fusiliers, who, according to Ernst Jünger in *Storm of Steel*, was personally buried by him in March 1917.

Continue over the bridge and immediately turn right. Continue down this road – running parallel with the motorway – for 500 metres until you reach a Y junction. Take the right hand road and follow it for 200 metres and stop (2)*.*

10e compagnie, 3e bataillon RMLE immediately prior to going 'over the top' at Belloy on 4 July 1916. This battalion was hit particularly badly over the next thirty-six hours and became ineffective as a fighting force by the time Belloy had been consolidated.

This was the front line on 4 July 1916 and the exact position from which the *Régiment de marche de la Légion étrangère* launched their attack on Belloy on that date.

Belloy was first occupied by the Germans on 29 August 1914; but they temporarily withdrew following the Battle of the Marne, returning during the Race to the Sea phase on 24 September. From this moment onwards they fortified the village, digging a network of electrically lit tunnels under the houses, reinforcing walls, carefully siting machine gun and observation positions and constructing trenches. As part of the German Second Line, they spent a year turning the village into a fortress and were so successful that the artillery preparation before the Battle of the Somme began did not weaken the defences at all. Following the fall of Dompierre, Fay and Assevillers, Belloy became the focal point of the German defence in this area and was the first main target for the *Division Marocaine*, which had just replaced the *3e Division d'infanterie coloniale* in the line.

Having relieved the *7e Régiment d'infanterie coloniale* at Assevillers during the early hours of 4 July, the *Régiment de marche de la Légion étrangère* waited in their front line trench (approximately following the road upon which you are now situated) opposite Belloy which was, at that time, under heavy bombardment.

View from the RMLE jump off trenches towards Belloy. It was in this field that Alan Seeger was mortally wounded.

The orders were to attack at 4am and to advance across the open wheat fields in two waves, with the objective of taking Belloy some 800 to 1,100 metres away. The first wave went into the attack in open order but, upon nearing the village, machine guns and rifles opened up from the remains of the buildings of the village, proving the ineffectiveness of the artillery preparation (or, alternatively, the effectiveness of over a year's worth of fortification). Two especially well sited positions, in the village cemetery and in a building just west of the town, created a devastating crossfire in the area about 200 metres west of the village. The first wave was cut down in swathes.

The second wave, upon witnessing the fate of the first, advanced more cautiously and, by the time they closed with the village, many were crawling through the wheat past the fallen bodies of their dead and wounded comrades.

The RMLE attack at Belloy, 4 July 1916.

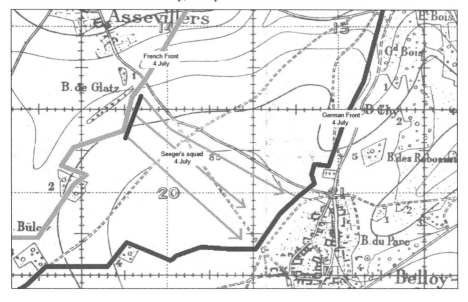

This wave, after hurling a hail of grenades on the outer defences, managed to break through into the village and launched a furious assault on the defences. Clearing the ruins by grenade and at bayonet point, house to house and hand to hand fighting continued for two hours until the village was finally cleared and the *Régiment de marche de la Légion étrangère* was established on the eastern edge of the village.

Throughout the night, the Germans launched ten counter-attacks in an attempt to retake the village. All were successfully beaten back and the line held until the regiment was relieved on 6 July.

During the fight for Belloy, the *Régiment de marche de la Légion étrangère* took over 750 German prisoners. However, they suffered the loss of twenty five officers and 844 other ranks (killed, wounded and missing). One of the more celebrated of these casualties was the American poet and writer Alan Seeger.

LM5157 Sdt 2 Cl Alan Seeger, *3e bataillon RMLE.*

Alan Seeger was born in New York on 22 June 1888. A Harvard graduate and resident of Paris by 1914, Seeger was in London at the time of the declaration of war. After returning to Paris soon afterwards, he enlisted into the *Légion étrangère* on 24 August 1914 and was allocated to the *2e Régiment de marche du 2er Régiment étrangère*, with whom he served in the Aisne, Vosges and Champagne sectors through 1915. After transferring to the *Régiment de marche de la Légion étrangère* following the amalgamations after the Second Battle of Champagne, Seeger only saw limited frontline service before being sent to the Somme as he was hospitalised with bronchitis between February and April 1916.

Part of the ill-fated first wave on 4 July 1916, Seeger was seen to fall after being hit in the stomach by machine gun fire outside the village. He managed to crawl into a shell hole and remove his equipment and great coat which he wrapped around himself in an attempt to use as a large dressing; but he was not found by the *brancardiers* (stretcher bearers) until several hours later. By this time, however, Seeger had died.

Along with the majority of the dead from this battle, Seeger's body was interred in the burial pits located at *Côtes 76* and *80* just outside Belloy. The remains from these pits were re-interred in the ossuaries of the *Nécropole nationale de Lihons* after the war and where now a small memorial to Seeger can be found.

One of his more famous poems, 'I have a Rendezvous with Death' – which was published posthumously in December 1916 – was a particular favourite of President John F Kennedy:

I have a rendezvous with Death
At some disputed barricade,
When Spring comes back with rustling shade
And apple-blossoms fill the air—
I have a rendezvous with Death
When Spring brings back blue days and fair.

It may be he shall take my hand
And lead me into his dark land
And close my eyes and quench my breath—
It may be I shall pass him still.
I have a rendezvous with Death
On some scarred slope of battered hill,
When Spring comes round again this year
And the first meadow-flowers appear.

God knows 'twere better to be deep
Pillowed in silk and scented down,
Where Love throbs out in blissful sleep,
Pulse nigh to pulse, and breath to breath,
Where hushed awakenings are dear ...
But I've a rendezvous with Death
At midnight in some flaming town,
When Spring trips north again this year,
And I to my pledged word am true,
I shall not fail that rendezvous.

Return to the Y junction and turn right towards Belloy, travelling in the same direction and over the same land as the attacking waves of the Régiment de marche de la Légion étrangère. As you approach the junction, notice the location of the village cemetery, where one of the most devastating machine guns was based, on the left. Turn right to visit the centre of **Belloy en Santerre (3).**

Plaques to Alan Seeger and Camil Campanya.

Belloy church. The church bells were donated by Seeger's parents in memory of their son.

The church bells of Belloy were donated to the village by the parents of Alan Seeger in memory of their son and, in response, his name appears on the village war memorial. There is also a plaque to Seeger on the wall of the building across from the war memorial, which sometimes has a floral tribute in the pattern of the Stars and Stripes of 'Old Glory'. Beneath this plaque is another plaque that commemorates one of Seeger's comrades – the Catalan poet **Camil Campanya** from Barcelona, who was also killed in the attack on Belloy on 4 July and who has no known grave. On the village green is an information panel telling the story of Seeger and, recently, another has appeared giving a brief history of Belloy-en Santerre's role during the Great War. The village war memorial itself has undergone a recent extensive restoration and addition and, though the base (including Seeger's name amongst the dead from the village) is original, the top part has been completely replaced to depict a *Poilu* of Great War vintage. Next to the village war memorial a new memorial was unveiled on the centenary of the battle for Belloy, 4 July 2016, commemorating the role of *La Légion étrangère* in the capture of Belloy.

Drive through Belloy and turn right onto the D79, then turn right onto the N29 towards Estrées.

On your right is the location of the Côte 76 and Côte 80 burial pits where Alan Seeger's body was first interred. In the immediate post war period, two French cemeteries were located along the N29 to the left of this junction and another was located on the right of the N29, just after the road to the motorway *péage* station before Estrées. This particular point marks the front line as it ran towards Estrées (facing in a southerly direction) from the evening of 4 July 1916 to the southerly attacks of September 1916.

*Upon entering **Estrées –Deniécourt**, turn left and then left again (this is the frontline position as from the end of July through to September) onto the D146 towards Berny-en-Santerre.*

The newly inaugurated RMLE memorial in Belloy.

Occupied by the Germans on 29 August 1914 (and then again, permanently, on 29 September 1914), Estrées was fortified by the

The new village war memorial and RMLE memorial in Belloy. As an adopted villager, Alan Seeger's name is listed amongst those of the dead from the village on the war memorial.

Germans throughout 1915 as part of the system protecting the area of Chaulnes from the north. The village was first entered by the *329e Régiment d'infanterie* on 4 July 1916, but could not be held; possession changed hands four times over the next two days. House by house, fighting continued throughout the few next weeks and it was not until 24 July that the village was completely in French possession. There is a **memorial to the *329e Régiment d'infanterie* (4)** and their actions of 4 and 5 July in the village.

Memorial to the *329e Régiment d'infanterie* at Estrées – Deniécourt.

In ***Berny en Santerre** (captured by the 4e Division d'infanterie on 17 September), turn left onto the D150 and back towards the N29. When this has been reached, turn right and follow the road until the **Nécropole nationale de Villers – Carbonnel** (5) can be seen on the left (it is possible to turn around on the roundabout in Villers Carbonnel if the road is too busy to cross).*

The **Nécropole nationale de Villers – Carbonnel** was created in 1920 following the concentration of French cemeteries at Barleux and Flaucourt. It was extended slightly by the Germans in 1941, with the reburial of French soldiers interred in the area from the May-June 1940

The Nécropole nationale de Villers – Carbonnel in 1920.

The Nécropole nationale de Villers – Carbonnel today.

period. Presently, the cemetery contains the remains of 2,285 French soldiers from the First World War (1,295 within the two ossuaries) and eighteen French soldiers from 1940.

Turn left at the Villers-Carbonnel roundabout onto the N17 (direction Péronne) but turn to the left onto the D148 after 350 meters. Follow this road through **Barleux (6)**, *turning right in the centre on to the D79.*

An anchor in the German defensive system south of Péronne, the frontline had arrived immediately west of Barleux by 5 July. Further attacks had pushed it nearer to the north of the village by 14 July, but the village itself remained steadfast. Directly assaulted by the *77e* and *15e Divisions d'infanterie* on 21 and 22 August, it was, again, attacked by them on 28 August, between 4 and 6 September and on 17 September. Throughout the remainder of the battle, however, the village held and did not fall until it was evacuated by the German Army during their withdrawal to the Hindenburg Line in 1917.

*After about two kilometres, you will start to get a good view of **La Maisonnette** (7), standing on the crest to your front left; you will pass one of the exit roads from this location after 2.7 kilometres.*

One of the most hotly contested sites on the whole of the 1916 Somme battlefield, La Maisonnette was a fortified farm and château located on high ground that gave dominating views over Péronne, the River Somme, the Flaucourt Plateau and much of the southern battlefield towards Belloy. Unseen movement on the eastern and northern faces of any sloping ground within five to six kilometres was difficult for the French while the Germans were still in occupation of this position. It was, therefore, imperative that La Maisonnette was taken.

The scene of two short, but vicious, actions in 1914 (28 August and 24 September), the 1916 battle arrived at La Maisonnette on 9 July following the fall of Biaches. Changing hands no less than fourteen times between this date and the end of the battle, it is believed that, per square metre, more shells fell on La Maisonnette than they did anywhere on the Verdun battlefield!

Originally taken by the *37e Régiment d'infanterie coloniale* and the *61e Bataillon de tirrailleurs sénégalais* during the afternoon of 9 July, the fighting was severe and casualties high. On this day the *37e* sustained 575 casualties, including 91 killed outright and 68 missing. The Senegalese lost 140 killed, 209 missing and 219 wounded. Relieved by the *35e Régiment d'infanterie coloniale* on 10 July, the position was lost again, then almost immediately regained, before the front was pushed to the eastern slope of the hill upon which La Maisonnette stands on 14 July. This line was then pushed back as far as Biaches during a German counter attack the following day, rendering La Maisonnette a front line outpost for both sides at varying times.

Fighting for La Maisonnette continued for the remainder of the Battle of the Somme, with particular fury during October. The position was lost for the final time by the French on 29 October. Though preparations were made, they never attempted to take it again.

Near the farm buildings at La Maisonnette was a memorial to the 56e Bataillon de chasseurs à pied, but, though it still appears to be marked on IGN maps, this was destroyed in 1994.

After the road drops down the hill, turn left at the junction onto the D1 towards Biaches.
[Note: Upon entering Biaches, it is possible to take the first left fork and then the first left turn to approach La Maisonnette, but it may be

Built on similar lines to its pre-war counterpart, the chateau of La Maisonnette as it looks today.

necessary to continue to drive past the farm and chateau and down the exit road back to the D79 and the entrance you passed earlier in order to continue the tour. However, if a good view of the location will suffice, then the following is recommended.]

In Biaches, take the first left turn before the Marie (take this turn very carefully, as there is a deep drainage gutter that is worse than any speed-bump!) and continue up the hill for 500 metres until Biaches village cemetery (8) is reached on your right.

Inside the communal cemetery is a mass grave containing the remains of thirty three *cuirassiers* from the *9e Régiment d'cuirassiers* and three unnamed Algerian *Goumiers*, who were killed at La Maisonnette on 24 September 1914. Alongside it (part of the same grave) is a headstone commemorating twelve *chasseurs* from the *7e Bataillon de chasseurs Alpin* who were killed there nearly a month earlier, on 28 August 1914. A good view of La Maisonnette farm and an appreciation of its commanding position can also be had from here.

Mass graves of the *9e Régiment d'cuirassiers*, the *7e Bataillon de chasseurs Alpin* and three unnamed Algerian *Goumiers* from 1914 in Biaches communal cemetery

A view across to the farm buildings of La Maisonnette from Biaches communal cemetery.

*Turn right, towards Flaucourt at the crossroads above the cemetery and pass a Y junction (500 metres) which was once home to a Coloniale memorial. After a further 500 metres, there is the tomb of **sous-Lieutenant Marcel Brocheriou** of the 22e Régiment d'infanterie coloniale on the grass banking to the right of the road (9). Parking here is difficult, but there is hard standing by the new wind turbines on the crest of the hill before the memorial.*

Sous-Lieutenant Marcel Brocheriou of the *22e Régiment d'infanterie coloniale.*

Marcel Henri Brocheriou was born at Arpagon, Seine-et-Oise on 13 March 1890. A career soldier, he served in the cavalry before gaining a commission into the colonial infantry and saw active service in North Africa prior to the war. A graduate of the academy at Saumur, he was killed in action between this location and Biaches on 6 August 1916.

The monument commemorating *Sous-Lieutenant* Marcel Brocheriou on the road to Flaucourt.

Continue down the road and, just before the village of Flaucourt is entered, a brick shelter can be seen in the field to the right **(10)**.

With a plaque carrying the words *Sur Ehre der/ fur Kaiser und Reich /Gefallen Söhne/ Deutschlands (In Honour of Germany's sons, Fallen for Kaiser and Reich)*, this is a rare survivor of a German built war time cemetery that once stood in the area of the German Second Line. Until the 1970s decaying wooden crosses still formed a semi-circle in front of this monument.

German commemorative monument located in the remains of the German war time cemetery at the entrance to Flaucourt.

Look to the west and north-westwards from the monument to see a good view of the Flaucourt Plateau and the open country across which the French would have to fight as from 4 July.

Continue into Flaucourt.

Practically abandoned on the night of the 2/3 July, the *23e Régiment d'infanterie coloniale* advanced in columns on the Second Line village of Flaucourt, with the *21e Régiment d'infanterie coloniale* to their immediate south, at 9am on the morning of 3 July. Relatively unopposed, they still managed to take 200 prisoners whilst clearing the cellars, dugouts and trenches up to the eastern fringe of the village. Out of the very low casualty list on this date one was particularly high profile. The regimental commander, *le lieutenant-colonel* Cambay, was wounded in a grenade accident in Flaucourt and had to be evacuated. *Chef de bataillon* Jouannetaud had to take command in his absence.

Turn right at the crossroads on to the D148 and head northwards following the front line of 3 - 4 July, which was located just beyond the buildings on your right.

After 1,200 metres turn right at the junction on to the D1 back towards Biaches

You are now traversing the **Flaucourt Plateau** in exactly the same direction and route at the *4e* and *24e Regiments d'infanterie coloniale* on the morning of 4 July 1916 as they pushed eastwards. Fighting through the communication trenches that ran parallel to the road whenever practicable in an attempt to remain as concealed from view as was possible on such open land, it took fourteen hours to advance the front by 1.7 kilometres. During this period, the *4e Regiment d'infanterie coloniale* took over 800 prisoners at a cost of sixty one deaths, eight missing and 330 wounded. The *24e Regiment d'infanterie coloniale*, slightly further to the north and away from the road, sustained sixty three casualties in total.

*After 1.7 kilometres, stop outside the **Nécropole nationale de Biaches** (11)*

The Nécropole nationale de Biaches. A front line position between 4 and 9 July 1916, a good appreciation of the expanse and openness of the Flaucourt Plateau upon which the cemetery stands can be had from this location.

186

You are now at the location where the front line remained steady from 4 to 9 July, running north – south across the road next to the cemetery. There were slight advances a few hundred metres north and south on 7 July, but the line in this spot remained stationary. Marking this point, the *Nécropole nationale de Biaches* was created in 1920 and extended in 1936. Like most of the French cemeteries, this was created by the concentration of several smaller French cemeteries and individual graves. Biaches contains graves from all over the Somme battlefield areas, but most graves date from 1916. It was listed as 'complete' in 1974 and contains the graves of 1,362 French soldiers from the First World War, including 322 who are interred in the two ossuaries.

Continue on the D1 into **Biaches**

Biaches marks the northernmost point on the south bank of the River where the line ran at the end of the Battle of the Somme 1916. It had been occupied by the Germans during their advance on 28 August 1914 and was vacated until after the Battle of the Marne. Returning to the area on 24 September 1914, the Germans converted it into a comfortable, but fortified, rear area village and light railway depot. Defended by a ring of trenches, overlooked by the positions at La Maisonnette and, just north of the road to Herbécourt, defended to the west by a complex redoubt system built around and including the ruins of an ancient fortified farm known as the *fortin de Biaches* (or the *ouvrage de Biache*), Biaches was a formidable target.

One of the objectives of the *72e Division d'infanterie* in an advance scheduled for 9 July, it fell to the *164e Régiment d'infanterie* to take the village itself. During an intense bombardment of the Biaches area, German guns on Mont St Quentin opened fire on the French line, causing many casualties and delaying the start time of the attack. Eventually, at 2pm, and in conjunction with the *16e Division d'infanterie coloniale's* attack on La Maisonnette, the assault was launched.

Coming under severe machine gun and artillery fire throughout, the village was reached by the companies advancing to the south of the Herbécourt road and fighting from house to house began as the French discovered pockets of resistance in nearly every other house. North of the road, the *9e* and *12e compagnies* had been held up by the *fortin de Biaches* and the *10e compagnie* (held in reserve) came forward to assist them, but were also pinned down.

By 6pm, Biaches had been all but taken (the final houses would eventually fall into French hands during the night and early hours of 9/10 July), but the *fortin* still held out and posed a serious threat to the French

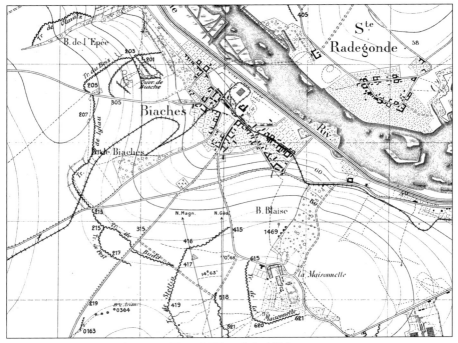

Biaches – La Maisonnette Trench Map, July 1916.

being able to defend against any serious counter attack. Attempts were made to mortar the position into silence, but it was too well entrenched and any hope of outflanking the position by moving along the bank of the Somme canal was dashed by the battery of machine guns watching the action from across the river near Ste Radegonde. An engineer officer was even consulted about the possibility of mining the position!

The following day, *capitaine* Vincendon offered to take a small patrol and attempt to take the *fortin* by surprise. At 2pm on 10 July, he set out, accompanied by a mixed bag of volunteers from the *9e* and *11e compagnies* and headquarters staff (*sous-lieutenant* Beaufort, *sergent* Mierut, *caporal* Thuin, *clairon* Detrait and *soldats* (*cyclistes*) Macquard, Martinet and Sellier). Splitting the group between himself and Beaufort, Vincendon led the two groups and crept down a communications trench into the *fortin* and both teams prepared themselves at either side of the central section of the position. After entering the heart of the *fortin* alone for reconnaissance purposes, Vincendon found no one in sight. Shouting into one of the dugouts, for the occupants to come out, the surprised Germans appeared and, on seeing the arrival of the two groups from two different directions, immediately surrendered, believing that they had been over-run.

The patrol returned to the French positions with two officers and 119 other ranks as prisoners. Each member of the patrol was awarded the *Croix de guerre* and cited in Army Orders. Vincendon's citation reads:

Officer of legendary courage. On 10 July 1916, at the head of a group of eight men, he had, with audacity, seized a fort occupied by an enemy company and three machine guns, which for twenty four hours had kept our troops in check, and made 114 prisoners, including two officers.

Biaches was finally in French hands and the *164e Régiment d'infanterie* was relieved on the evening of 10 July. Pushing as far as the eastern side of Bois Blaise and just a kilometre short of the Somme river crossing at Péronne by the evening of 14 July 1916, the Germans launched a furious counter-attack on Biaches (and La Maisonnette) on 15 July and again on the 17 July during which they recaptured the village. They were, however, driven out of most of the village again on 19 July and the front line remained through the centre of Biaches for the rest of the battle: Biaches church marked the position of the German front line from the end of July 1916 until the withdrawal of 1917.

Biaches church – photograph taken from the canal bank. This location -from the position of the photograph to the right of the church – marks the exact position of the German front line at the end of the Battle of the Somme.

189

Continue through Biaches until the N17 is reached. A left turn will take you into Péronne centre or a right turn will take you back to Villers-Carbonnel, where turning right onto the N29 will eventually take you back to Foucaucourt en Santerre, where the next tour is best begun.

GPS Waypoints, Tour 2 Part 2

1 - 49°53'47.44"N, 2°50'33.03"E   2 - 49°53'17.95"N, 2°50'35.83"E
3 - 49°52'57.32"N, 2°51'20.44"E   4 - 49°52'30.89"N, 2°49'19.93"E
5 - 49°52'35.06"N, 2°53'35.96"E   6 - 49°53'44.96"N, 2°53'33.86"E
7 - 49°54'56.91"N, 2°54'45.16"E   8 - 49°55'15.00"N, 2°54'15.05"E
9 - 49°55'3.44"N, 2°53'24.29"E   10 - 49°54'43.99"N, 2°52'1.63"E
11 - 49°55'39.01"N, 2°53'13.80"E

End of Tour 2

Tour 3: The southernmost battle
September – December 1916

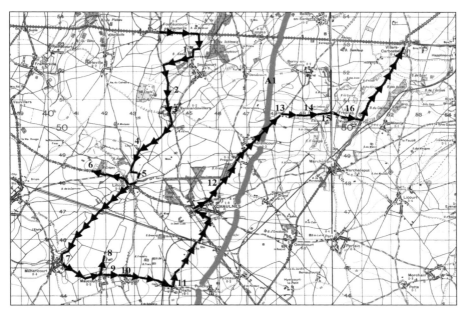

Tour 3.

START: **Foucaucourt en Santerre**

*On the N29 through Foucaucourt, travel eastwards for 1.4 kilometres. At the first crossroads after leaving the village and before Bois Satyre is reached, turn right and follow the road to Wallieux. Turn left through the hamlet and then right before the village of **Soyécourt** is reached.*

A pair of German held front line villages since the end of September 1914, Wallieux and Soyécourt were not directly involved in the opening months of the Somme battle, even though they were a mere 300 to 400 metres south of the most southerly attacking unit. There was increasingly aggressive patrol activity, localised (mainly German) attacks in the area, heavy shelling and a slightly southerly movement of the front line between 10 and 20 July designed to ease pressure on the French troops

191

holding the southern flank of the offensive. This made Wallieux a front line hamlet, both on its northern and its western fringes, but it was not until September and the extension of the French offensive southwards that it and Soyécourt had any real involvement in the fighting raging just to their north.

Both villages were captured by the *43e Division d'infanterie* on 4 September 1916 after an intense artillery bombardment. At 2pm, following a creeping barrage that was laid down 200 metres forward of the attacking waves, they were seized in a single rush directed towards Deniécourt, taking the German line that ran in front of the villages and Bois Keman (Wallieux Wood).

The *149e Régiment d'infanterie,* along with the *3e Bataillon de chasseurs à pied* to their left, managed to advance two kilometres beyond Soyécourt and onto the ridge overlooking Ablaincourt; but they had to pull back as they were badly exposed because of the failure of the attacks that took place at Vermandovillers and Deniécourt. This left them vulnerable to machine gun cross-fire and shelling from three directions. After withdrawing to the area between the southern edge of Soyécourt and the château's park in Deniécourt, the units involved consolidated their positions.

The small wooded area on your right is **Bois Keman** (**1**).

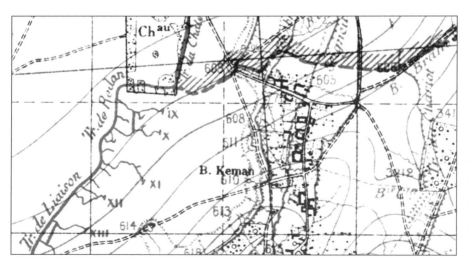

Bois Keman Trench Map, July 1916.

This is a preserved area of woodland that has been opened to visitors. A well constructed walkway has been provided through a small section of the wood from which shellholes, trenches and collapsed underground workings are all clearly visible. Captured along with Wallieux and Soyécourt on 4 September, this wood had been a front line position for two years at the time of its capture. The German front ran along the wood's western edge in a north-south direction, with the French front running parallel to it some 600 metres across the field to the west.

Preserved trenches and dug outs in Bois Keman today.

The German military cemetery of Vermandovillers in the 1920s.

*Continue along this road, crossing the No Man's Land of 4 September at a slight angle, to the junction and turn left on to the D143 towards Vermandovillers. This junction marks the position of the French front line trench. After 820 metres and just over the motorway bridge, pull off the D143 on to the side road (the original D143); this is **Vermandovillers German Cemetery (2)**.*

Holding the remains of 22,632 German soldiers, Vermandovillers is the largest military cemetery on the Somme and is still open for burials. It was created by the French army in 1920, based on an existing war time cemetery, concentrating remains from numerous other cemeteries and individual graves from all across the Somme battlefields (and even further afield). The majority of burials date from the 1916 and 1918 Battles of the Somme; of those from the 1914-15 period, many were interred in the original cemetery (though one small 1914-15 cemetery was moved here from the Arras sector). The German War Graves Commission (*Volksbund Deutsche Kriegsgräberfürsorge*) took over the care of the cemetery in 1927.

There are 9,455 individual graves in the cemetery, of which 379 are of unknown German soldiers. Nearly 13,200 are buried in the 15 *kameradengraben* mass-graves. Two notable interments are those of the dramatist and poet **Reinhard Johannes Sorge**, who died of wounds caused by an exploding grenade at the age of 24 near Ablaincourt on 20 July 1916; and

Reinhard Johannes Sorge.

194

The largest (by interments) military cemetery on the Somme – Vermandovillers German cemetery today.

the expressionist writer **Alfred Lichtenstein**, who was killed in action, aged 25, near Vermandovillers on 25 September 1914. Both are now buried in the *kameradengraben*.

Alfred Lichtenstein.

900 metres across the road, to the west of the southern section of the cemetery is the site of **Bois Etoilé**, of which only the southern part now remains; even so, it still remains an extensive expanse of woodland. This was the site of a stand by the *75e Régiment d'infanterie* on 24 September 1914 that forced the Germans to dig in. The German line became established on its western fringe and remained in this area for the next two years. Bois Etoilé was a primary objective for the *132e Division d'infanterie* during the attacks at Vermandovillers between 4 and 9 September 1916. Though Bois Etoilé was taken, Vermandovillers remained in German hands. It would be with an attack from the eastern side of the wood that the battle for Vermandovillers would continue into late September.

Heavily defended, with deep trenches and concrete machine gun emplacements, many of these remains can still be found in the wood. However, like so many Somme woods, it is private property and permission to enter must be sought first.

*Return to the main road and continue into **Vermandovillers** (3).*

Attacked by the *132e Division d'infanterie* on 4 September as part of the general offensive in this area, the defences of Vermandovillers proved an impossible obstacle to overcome. Though the Bois Etoilé fell on the first day, this was the only success and the battle dragged on for a further five days with no great progress, other than the *1e Bataillon de chasseurs à pied* managing to push forward and hold the ground in front of the village cemetery on 6 September. The French infantry having suffered from heavy losses throughout this period, the attacks were temporarily called off as the artillery began the preparation work for further assaults, systematically destroying the village with large calibre rounds. Retaliatory fire from German guns ensured that there could not be much movement in the open and several units were rotated through the sector. After putting Vermandovillers under heavy bombardment for a full week, the next attempt was scheduled for 17 September.

The attack was launched on the 17th, with the *120e Division d'infanterie* now in the line. Directly opposite Vermandovillers, the *86e Régiment d'infanterie* moved forward into the assault at 3pm, sending one battalion to the north of the village to clear the concrete defensive system located in the houses there with grenades; the village was finally secured by evening. Some heavy losses were incurred in the area of Bois du Cerisier, some 500 metres to the east of the village, due to machine guns located in that copse not being targeted by the artillery; but these were eventually knocked out and the village held.

*On the left, just beyond the crossroads in the centre of the Vermandovillers and next to the church, are two memorials. One is to the **1e Bataillon de chasseurs à pied** and commemorates their actions in the area between August and December 1916. It also has an attached individual commemoration to **chasseur François Lamy**.. Next to it is a memorial to **Capitaine Jean Delcroix** of the 327e Régiment d'infanterie, who was killed in action outside Vermandovillers on 6 September 1916. Another monument in the Place du Souvenir nearby commemorates **Pierre Victoire Bourguet** and the 158e Régiment d'infanterie in their actions at the Boyeau du Duc on 6 - 9 September.*

François Henri Lamy served as a *soldat 2e classe* in the *1e Bataillon de chasseurs à pied*. He was born at Loudes, Haute-Loire, on 15 July 1886 and was a farmer before the war. He embarked upon his (compulsory) military service with the *28e Bataillon de chasseurs à pied* in October 1907 and was recalled for war service on 2 August 1914. Transferred to

The memorials to *Capitaine* **Jean Delcroix of the** *327e Régiment d'infanterie* **and the** *1e Bataillon de chasseurs à pied* **(with individual plaque to** *chasseur* **François Lamy).**

the *1e Bataillon de chasseurs à pied* on 5 May 1915, François saw action near Arras during the Second Battle of Artois and at Verdun before arriving on the Somme. He was killed in action near the communal cemetery of Vermandovillers on 6 September 1916.

Jean Léon Florimond Delcroix was from Douai, Nord. Born on 24 April 1890, he was killed in action during an attack on trenches in front of Bois de Chaulnes, south of Vermandovillers, on 6 September 1916.

Pierre Victorin Bourguet was an *aspirant* in the *7e compagnie* of the *158e Régiment d'infanterie* when he was killed in action on 8 September 1916 near Bois du Page at Vermandovillers. His sons arranged for this memorial to be erected in 2000.

Continue through Vermandovillers on the D143 to the roundabout and take the first right on to the D79 (direction Lihons). After 1.5 kilometres, the road bends to the left. On the right hand side of the road on this bend is **Lihu Ferme (4).**

A heavily fortified strongpoint in the French line since September 1914, Lihu Farm today.

A pivotal defensive point for the French Army following the loss of Chaulnes on 24 September 1914, this ancient fortified farm formed part of the northern defences of Lihons. A formidable and almost perfect defensive position, the farm buildings were also protected to the north, south and west by the woodland of Grand Bois, which no longer exists.

After conducting a fighting retreat from Chaulnes, the *52e* and *140e Régiments d'infanterie* reached the thick walls of Lihu Ferme and the outskirts of Lihons and, under fire, began to improve the defences and entrenched the area around Lihu Farm and Grand Bois, continuing these southwards to meet up with the defences of Lihons. Unable to proceed any further, the Germans began to dig in opposite. Several French attempts to recapture Chaulnes, from 29 September 1914, proved disastrous. Sporadic but severe fighting continued in this area throughout the remainder of 1914, including a large scale attack on the Lihons brick works on Christmas Eve, Christmas Day and Boxing Day 1914, and all through 1915; the line remained static here until the later stages of the Battle of the Somme in 1916. By 1916 Lihu Farm had been reduced to nothing more than a ruin and remained in French hands until the German offensives of 1918.

After 800 metres the road swings to the right at the town cemetery (on the left). Take the small road to the left in front of the cemetery then, after 160 metres, turn left. At the T junction at the end of this short stretch, in the woodland to your left front, can be located the the **tomb of Prince Murat (5).**

198

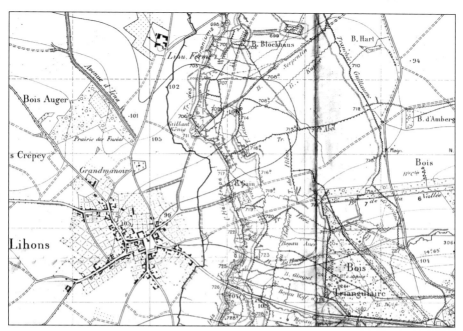

Lihons Trench Map, April 1916.

Surmounted by the Napoléonic eagle, the tomb of Prince Murat is near to the location of his death at Lihons.

199

Louis Marie Michel Joachim Napoléon Murat, Prince Murat, was born on 8 September 1896 in Rocquencourt, Yvelines. The great-great grandnephew of Napoléon I, Emperor of France, and the great great grandson of Napoléon's sister, Caroline Bonaparte, and her husband Joachim Murat, Prince Louis enlisted into the *5e Régiment de cuirassiers à pied* in April 1915 and saw service on the Champagne front before arriving on the Somme, by which time he had been appointed to the rank of *maréchal des logis* (sergeant). Just four days after his arrival at the front in this sector, Prince Louis was killed in action on 21st August 1916 by the detonation of a rifle grenade near this spot, which is just behind the French front line trench of 1914-16. His family decided to bury him where he fell. The small parkland in which Prince Louis' tomb in located was purchased by the Murat family and donated to the town of Lihons in 1961. There are streets named in honour of Louis Murat in Lihons and Paris.

Prince Louis Marie Michel Joachim Napoléon Murat. Though of distinctive lineage, he was serving as a *maréchal des logis* (sergeant in the cavalry) in the *5e Régiment de cuirassiers à pied* at the time of his death.

Within this small park, there is also a memorial stone erected by the *5e Régiment de cuirassiers* in honour of the **Poles who served France** in the armies of Louis XV, and for the men who served ion the regiment during the 1870-71 War, in 1914-18, in 1939-45, in Indochina and in Algeria.

Behind the tomb, the remains of old quarries mark the site of the **Lihons Briqueterie** and the location of the 'Christmas Battle' of 1914.

From your last position take the (rough) road to the right for 200 metres, running parallel with the 1916 French front that was some ninety metres to your left, and then right again. After 300 metres, you will have reached the D337. Turn right through **Lihons** *and, continuing on the D337, you will arrive at the* **Nécropole nationale de Lihons** *(6) on the right, some 1,200 metres from the town centre.*

Begun by the French Army in January 1915, the *cimetiére des Pommiers* was used throughout the war by the French Army and then, during their occupation of this area, the British. It was enlarged in 1919 by the concentration of smaller cemeteries from the Somme battlefields and again in 1935-36 by the relocation of individual graves, other small cemeteries and some of those buried in communal cemeteries. Many of the graves from the areas of Framerville-Rainecourt, Herleville,

The Nécropole nationale de Lihons.

Foucaucourt-en-Santerre, Harbonnières, Assevillers, Belloy-en-Santerre, Cayeux-en-Santerre, Le Quesnel and Fontaine-lès-Cappy are now located here. Presently, the cemetery contains the remains of 6,581 French soldiers (including 1,638 in four ossuaries), four British (of whom two are unknown) and one Canadian.

Many of the remains of the fallen from the attack of the *Régiment de marche de la Légion étrangère* on Belloy-en-Santerre on 4 July 1916 are now interred here, so, though they are officially 'French' casualties, an interesting array of nationalities are to be found in this cemetery: Spaniards, Poles, Danes, Swiss, Italians, Americans, Swedes, Russians, etc.

Ossuary No.1 at the rear of the cemetery almost certainly contains the remains of Alan Seeger and a plaque dedicated to him, including lines from his poem 'Bellenglise', was unveiled at the cemetery entrance just after the 90th anniversary of his death in 2006.

Ossuary number one - the probable final resting place of Alan Seeger.

Seeger plaque at the cemetery entrance with lines from his poem 'Bellenglise'.

*Return to Lihons on the D337 and turn right onto the D131 (direction Méharicourt). Take the first left upon entering **Méharicourt (7)**, then the left fork and left again onto the D39 (direction Maucourt).*

In Allied hands from September 1914 to March 1918, Méharicourt was the location of several dressing stations and headquarters for units serving in this sector. A hub for troops moving into (and out of) the line at Maucourt – no less than five communications trenches led directly to the front from this village, it was regularly shelled and gassed. Some sources state that it was actually in this area that phosgene was first encountered on 28th November 1915.

Continue on the D39 to Maucourt.

A French front line village from 1914 to 1916, this was the most southerly point of the 1916 Somme battle. With the area occupied by the *20e Division d'infanterie*, the battle was joined here on 4 September. Following six days of bombardment, the *25e Régiment d'infanterie* left their trenches on the eastern edge of the village at 2pm with the *136e Régiment d'infanterie* on their right, the southernmost attacking unit in the entire battle, and the *2e Régiment d'infanterie* on their left. Though the *25e* was stopped dead in their tracks in front of the village of Chilly by the massed machine guns located in concrete emplacements that had survived the terrific bombardment, the *2e* succeeded in the capture of

Bois Fréderic and Bois Browning to the north and the *136e* broke through the first two lines of German trenches to the south, effectively encircling Chilly. Elements of the *25e* moved north and south, enveloping the village and, eventually, managed to remove the obstacles from the sides and rear and capture the village. After three days of fending off German counter-attacks, further advances in this area proved impossible and the line remained static until end of the Somme Offensive three months later.

*In the centre of the village, turn left at the crossroads and drive past the village cemetery to the **Nécropole nationale de Maucourt** (8).*

The Nécropole nationale de Maucourt.

Situated on the old road to Lihons, the *Nécropole nationale de Maucourt* was constructed in 1920 by the concentration of graves found on the southern Somme battlefield and transferring the men buried in the French military cemetery at Méharicourt. Further extensions were made to the cemetery in 1935, 1936 and between 1949 and 1953.

Currently the cemetery contains the remains of 5,302 French and British servicemen, including 1,534 interred in the six ossuaries. 5,272 are French soldiers from the First World War, but twenty four French soldiers who fell in 1940 were buried here between 1949 and 1953. In the south-western corner of the cemetery, close to the road, are the graves of six airmen (five from the Royal Air Force and one from the Royal Canadian Air Force), who were the crew members of a bomber shot down on 17 April 1943.

In the early 2000s it was planned to build an international airport on this site but, due to protests and a change of government, the project was eventually abandoned. Should this plan have ever come to fruition, it would also have signalled the destruction of the village of Vermandovillers and the necessity to relocate the huge German cemetery there as well as the French cemeteries of Maucourt and, possibly, Lihons.

Return to the crossroads and turn left.

At the exit of the village of Maucourt is a **memorial to the *7e* and *14e* Bataillons Alpin de chasseurs à pied** and the ***5e Régiment d'infanterie* (9)**, commemorating their actions here in September and October 1914.

The original memorial to the 1914 actions of the *7e* and *14e* *Bataillons Alpin de chasseurs à pied* and the *5e Régiment d'infanterie* at the exit of Maucourt village. Marking the position of the French front line of 1914-1916 the current, rather dilapidated, memorial replaced the one depicted in this image some years ago.

The road will now take you over the No Man's Land of 1914-16 to **Chilly (10).**

In Chilly – the southernmost village captured during the Battle of the Somme (captured by the *136e Régiment d'infanterie* on 4 September 1916) – there can still be seen the remains of several of the concrete emplacement that held up the attackers that afternoon as you approach the village in the same direction of the attack, including a magnificently preserved example in the field in front of the farm on the left on the slight right hand bend as you enter the village. There are also the remains of a later dated (October /November 1916) French observation post near the first road junction inside the village.

The main street of Chilly following its capture in September 1916.

*Continue towards **Hallu** (11)*

600 metres after leaving Chilly, look up a farm track to the left. The copse that you can see across the field some 500 metres from the road is Bois Fréderic, captured by *2e Régiment d'infanterie* on 4 September 1916. The south and east edges of this copse mark the location of the French front here from that date until the conclusion of the Battle of the Somme.

The road continues, crossing the German front line 120 metres after the farm track, into the village of Hallu

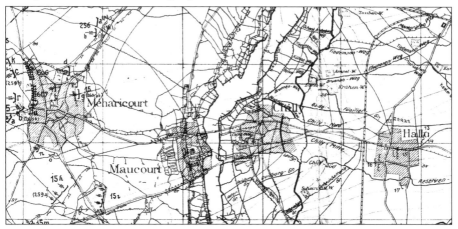

Maucourt – Chilly Trench Map, July 1916.

Hallu, after the September 1916 actions, became a German front line village. It remained German held until the withdrawals of March 1917.

At the main crossroads in Hallu, turn left on to the D132 towards **Chaulnes**.

A heavily fortified town in the German Second Line, Chaulnes was one of the objectives for the general attack of 4 September. By 7 September, the direct frontal assault by the *26e Division d'infanterie* from the direction of Lihons had been stopped in its tracks some 500 metres short of its target and the front settled until the next attempt on 10 October. Though some progress was made to the north, the attack, again, stalled. This time the Bois de Chaulnes (with its numbered segments) proved to be too much of an obstacle. Although a foothold was gained on the 10th, the *51e Division d'infanterie* failed to complete the capture of the town the following day and, in the course of a German counter-attack, a battalion of the *25e Régiment d'infanterie* was almost totally destroyed. Fighting continued unabated within these woods (especially in Bois 4, which has been compared to the fighting for Delville Wood in the British sector) until the next attack on 21 October. Though some gains were made

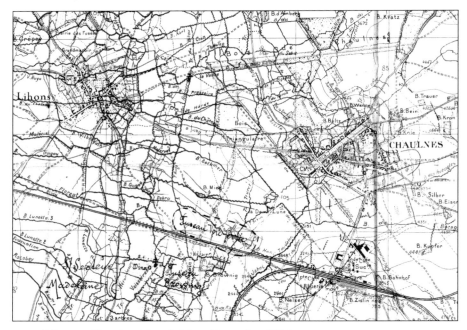

Lihons – Chaulnes Trench Map, November 1916.

206

– mainly through the element of surprise – a strong German counter-attack on 22 October restored the fighting line to its 21 October positions. The struggle would continue for several more weeks, with small scale and short distance confrontations and one major attack on 7 November.

A final attempt to capture Chaulnes took place on 5 December 1916 (the final action of the Battle of the Somme in the French sector). The attack involved an assault on and the capture of Chaulnes by attacking the north and north east of the town in a joint thrust conducted by the *183e* and *184e Brigades d'infanterie*; whilst an eastwardly directed assault went in from the south, aiming to encircle the town and capturing Hallu and the Chaulnes railhead in the process. In the semi frozen mud, this attempt also bogged down in failure. Another attempt, scheduled for later in December, was called off at the last minute when Général Nivelle halted all further offensive actions, effectively ending the Battle of the Somme on 17 December 1916.

*Once Chaulnes is reached, turn left at the roundabout (D337)and proceed for 600 metres before turning right (direction Ablaincourt and Marchélepot). At the Y Junction after 650 metres, take the left hand road (the D150) towards Ablaincourt, skirting the front line wood, **Bois Kratz** (12). Just before the wood is reached, look to the left. 800 metres across the field is the woodland that, once part of the Bois de Chaulnes, was known as Bois 4.*

Scene of some of the most intensive woodland fighting in the area – and some of the last actions of the Battle of the Somme – Bois de Chaulnes.

Part of the woodland protecting the northern approach to Chaulnes, only the northern part of Bois Kratz was ever captured and retained. The position where the road bends slightly to the left, a hundred metres before the end of the wood, marks the location of the final French line (running left to right across your front) of December 1916.

*Continue through **Pressoir** and **Ablaincourt** (both captured on 7 November by the 62e Division d'infanterie, who was still in occupation to defend these locations against a massive German counter-attack on 15 November) and cross the TGV line and motorway. 700 metres beyond the motorway, turn right at the crossroads (the location of the **sucrerie de Génermont** in 1916)* **(13)**.

Site of the sucrerie de Génermont, captured by the *17e Régiment d'infanterie* on 14 October 1916.

After one kilometre, look to the left.

In this empty field and at this exact spot, the main section of the hamlet of **Génermont (14)** once stood (a row of buildings also lined the road to your right). Continue 150 metres to the crossroads with a crucifix on the left. The village cemetery of Génermont was located a hundred metres up the track beyond the crucifix and about forty metres into the field to the left. This was also used as a front line cemetery by French soldiers.

The site of the hamlet of Génermont. Nothing but fields remain today.

Génermont whilst still in German occupation during the early autumn of 1916.

Captured, along with the *sucrerie de Génermont*, by the *17e Régiment d'infanterie* in a brilliantly executed assault from the north and north west on 14 October 1916, the tiny hamlet of Génermont remained located just behind the French front line for the remainder of the battle. Part of the failed 7 November assault from the north towards the Amiens-Péronne railway, Marchélepot and the attack to the north of Chaulnes was launched from here but, both being failures, the line as it was in mid October remained so for the rest of the battle. Located a mere 300 metres behind the front line of October 1916 – March 1917, Génermont was shelled out of existence. Nothing remains of the hamlet today other than the name of the field.

Modern aerial photograph showing the site of Génermont with the location of the hamlet's buildings and cemetery superimposed.

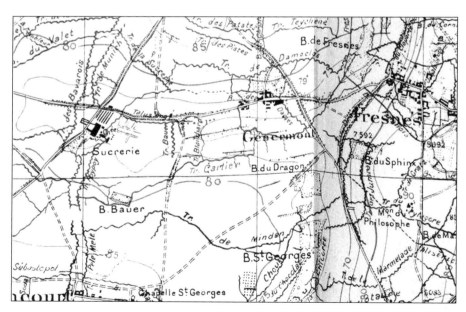

Génermont – Fresnes Trench Map, October 1916.

210

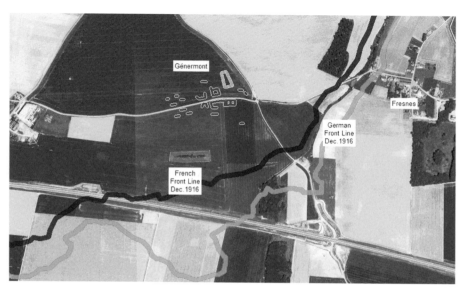

Modern aerial photograph showing the site of Génermont with the location of the final front lines at the end of the Battle of the Somme superimposed.

Continue over the crossroads, past the (French) front line woodland of **Bois de Fresnes** **(15)**. *The final front line ran northwards here, along the road to your left in front of the wood's eastern edge. Continue on the D45E through the (German) front line village of* **Fresnes –Mazancourt** **(16)**.

The site of the December 1916 German front line at Fresnes.

Upon arrival at the crossroads with the N17, turn left towards Péronne. After 3.3 kilometres, the roundabout at Villers – Carbonnel is reached, with its choice of directions.

GPS Waypoints, Tour 3

1 - 49°52'2.55"N, 2°47'29.64"E   2 - 49°51'21.61"N, 2°46'54.72"E
3 - 49°51'0.08"N, 2°46'56.52"E   4 - 49°50'9.20"N, 2°46'8.05"E
5 - 49°49'41.97"N, 2°46'14.62"E   6 - 49°49'40.20"N, 2°44'53.08"E
7 - 49°47'53.60"N, 2°43'56.79"E   8 - 49°48'0.05"N, 2°45'17.90"E
9 - 49°47'41.26"N, 2°45'24.78"E   10 - 49°47'43.30"N, 2°46'0.97"E
11 - 49°47'35.06"N, 2°47'20.37"E   12 - 49°49'38.52"N, 2°48'39.42"E
13 - 49°51'2.56"N, 2°50'18.26"E   14 - 49°51'4.19"N, 2°51'10.53"E
15 - 49°51'6.56"N, 2°51'35.43"E   16 - 49°51'7.87"N, 2°51'47.66"E

End of Tour 3

Appendix One

The French Cemeteries on the Somme

Within the zone of the 1916 Battle of the Somme, there are scattered eighteen French *Nécropoles Nationales* (though one of these is specific to the 1914 actions and another to 1915), containing the remains of *at least* 55,303 French soldiers from the 1914-18 war, the majority of which date from the 1916 battle. This figure does not include those who are buried in other *Cimetières militaries* that are not designated as *Nécropoles Nationales* (such as the French cemetery at Éclusier-Vaux, which contains over a hundred French graves), those that are interred in cemeteries that (are now) under the care of the Commonwealth War Graves Commission (such as the 120 Frenchmen buried in Ovillers Military Cemetery and the 300 French burials at Thiepval Anglo-French Cemetery), those interred in the military sections of communal cemeteries - *carrés militaries*- or those buried in individual and/or private graves.

Another factor to bear in mind when looking for the final resting places of the French dead from the Battle of the Somme is that the French had a policy of repatriation of her war dead if requested by and, until 1946, at the expense of the next of kin, meaning that many hundreds of the fallen from the Somme are scattered throughout France in local cemeteries and *carrés militaries*. One such example is that of **Soldat Georges Desiré Brochart** of the *365e Régiment d'infanterie*.

A barber's assistant from Roubaix in the Nord region, Georges enlisted for his compulsory military service as a 21 year old at Lille on 15 November 1903 and served with the *106e Régiment d'infanterie* as part of the Verdun garrison until September 1906, when he was transferred to the reserve and returned home to his civilian life (transferring to the *165e Régiment d'infanterie* as a reservist in 1913). Recalled for war service on 12 August 1914, he re-entered the army with the *365e Régiment d'infanterie* (the reserve regiment of the *165e*) and saw action on the Wöevre and the Meuse Heights in 1914 and spent much of 1915 in the Verdun sector. Engaged in battle during the first week of the Verdun offensive in February 1916, his regiment then moved to the Vosges before transferring to the Somme in June 1916, where he was in reserve on the opening day. After moving forward towards Feuilléres on 4 July, Georges was severely wounded in the Bois du Chapitre, just south

The *Livret Militaire* of *Soldat* Georges Desiré Brochart of the *365e Régiment d'infanterie*, who was severely wounded near Feuilléres on 7 July and died at Villers-Bretonneux the following day. Along with his *plaques d'identité* (of which two had been on issue to each French soldier since May 1915), the *Livret Militaire* was the main identity document carried by a French soldier and could be found on his person at all times.

of Feuilléres on 7 July and medically evacuated. He died of wounds in hospital at Villers-Bretonneux on 8 July 1916 and was buried there later that same day.

At his family's request, however, Georges' remains were moved to his home town after the war and he is now at rest in the *carré militaire* of the town cemetery at Roubaix, where he is buried alongside his younger brother, Lucien, who was killed in action at Venteuil, Marne on 21 July 1918 whilst serving with the *102e Régiment d'infanterie* during the Bataille de Reims 1918.

The care of the French *Nécropoles Nationales*, though not necessarily of *carrés militaries*, currently falls under the jurisdiction of the *Service des sépultures de guerre* part of the *Ministère des anciens combattants et victimes de guerre* section of the *Ministère de la defence,* which can trace its history back to the formation of the *Service Général des Pensions* on 18 February 1916. Following on from a law passed on 29 December 1915, in which the right to a perpetual resting place on French soil for any soldier in the French or Allied armies who had died for or in defence of France was granted, this government department was established to deal with the pensions of surviving soldiers and their next of kin and the burials of the enormous number of casualties that had been suffered up to then. Prior to this, the care and maintenance of war graves had been left to individuals, communities, regiments and organisations, such as the

Georges Brochart's grave in the *carré militaire* of Roubaix municiple cemetery. Note that the headstone does not follow the same uniform patterns that are found in the *Nécropoles Nationales* that are maintained by the *Service des sépultures de guerre*. This is a common feature of *carrés militaries* throughout France.

Souvenir Français; this organisation had been maintaining memorials and war graves and perpetuating the memory of fallen soldiers since 1872, but had found it difficult to cope with the scale of casualties incurred since the start of the war.

On 25 November 1918, a national commission for military graves – the *Service des sépultures de guerre* - was established to oversee the reorganisation of French military cemeteries and establish a standard architectural and horticultural style. Each cemetery was to be laid out with a central pathway, including a flagpole for the national flag. Concrete Latin crosses or marker stones of varying shape, dependent on the religious faith of the fallen soldier, were to replace original grave markers and, as all graves were intended to be identical, no grave was to be embellished in any way more than another. Individual and unit

215

memorials were permitted, however, and many cemeteries contain these. Mass graves (ossuaries) also feature in many cemeteries and contain the final resting places of many known and unknown dead. Those interred in the ossuaries whose identities are known are always listed on name panels. During the reconstruction of the French cemeteries after the war, gravel was laid and the mound of each grave was marked by a border of carnations. In the late 1930s and during the 1950s, grass lawns and plants were introduced to the cemeteries. The polyanthas rose was the most commonly adopted flower as it flowered abundantly, with red blooms, from the spring to the early frosts of autumn. Decorative landscaping with trees and shrubs has been carried out in some cemeteries more recently and many of the concrete grave markers have been replaced with a more hard wearing plastic compound. Inside the entrance gate of most cemeteries can be found a box containing the cemetery plan and register and, often, a visitors book. Recent additions to the *Nécropoles Nationales* include information panels that detail the wartime and post-war history of the particular area and cemetery and also list the other *Nécropoles Nationales* that may be able to found in the vicinity.

French *Nécropoles Nationales* on the 1916 Somme Battlefield
Albert:
Creation date: 1923
6,293 French burials, including 2,879 buried within four ossuaries
3 British burials
Contains the remains of soldiers who died throughout the actions on the Somme from 1914-18 and is a concentration of small cemeteries from across the entire Somme *département*.

Amiens *'Saint Acheul'*:
Creation date: Wartime Cemetery. Exact date not known (1914-18)
2,739 French burials, 10 Belgian, 12 British and 1 Russian from the Battles of the Somme 1914-18
12 French burials from 1939-45
Extended in 1921 and 1935 with exhumations from cemeteries in the areas of Conty, Thoix, Boves and Cagny.

Amiens *'Saint Pierre'*:
Creation date: Wartime Cemetery. Exact date not known (1914-18)
1,347 French and 25 Belgian burials from 1914-18
Extended in 1921 and 1934 with exhumations from around Amiens, Dury and La Madeleine

Beaumont-Hamel *'Cimetière de Serre-Hébuterne'*:
Creation date: 1919. Constructed by the Imperial War Graves Commission and maintained by them into the 1930s
834 French burials, including 240 in the ossuary. Mainly from the combats at Hébuterne of June 1915.
Extended between 1919 and 1923 with the concentration of graves from the *243e* and *327e Régiments d'infanterie*

Biaches:
Creation date: Wartime cemetery. 1916-18
1,362 French burials from the Battles of the Somme, including 322 within two ossuaries.
Extended in 1920 and 1936 with the concentration of smaller cemeteries from across the entire Somme *department*. Closed for further burials in 1974

Bray-sur-Somme:
Creation date: Wartime Cemetery. Exact date not known (1914-18)
1,044 French burials, including 102 in an ossuary
1 British burial.
Extended in 1923 and 1935 with concentrations from cemeteries in front of Bray and Suzanne. Closed for further burials in 1990.

Cerisy:
Creation date: Wartime cemetery. 1916
990 French burials.
Extended in 1923 with the concentration of bodies from the *carré militaire* of the communal cemetery at Cerisy. Closed for further burials during 1979-80.

Clery-sur-Somme *' Le Bois des Ouvrages'*:
Creation date: 1920
2,332 French burials including 1,129 buried in two ossuaries.
Extended in 1920 and 1936 with burials exhumed from the sectors of Monacu Farm, Fargny Mill, bois de Berlingots and *carrés militaires* at Morlancourt and Vaires-sous-Corbie.

Dompierre-Becquincourt:
Creation date: 1920
7,032 French burials, including 1,671 buried in four ossuaries.
1 German burial from 1914-18 and 1 French from 1939-45

Extended in 1920, 1935 and 1936 with the concentration of various cemeteries from across the Somme. Individual graves and remains discovered between 1948 and 1985 were also buried here.

Etinehem *'La Côte 80'*:
Creation date: Wartime Cemetery. Exact date not known (1914-18)
955 French burials, 49 British
Extended in 1923 with the concentration of remains from the cemeteries between Etinehem and Méricourt-sur-Somme. Contains the personal headsone marking the grave of *l'abbé* Thibaut, regimental chaplain (*aumonier*) of the *1e Régiment d'infanterie*, who was killed in action on 26 September 1916.

Hattencourt:
Creation date: 1920
1,942 French burials, including 667 buried in four ossuaries
2 Russians from 1914-18 and 5 French from 1939-45
Extended in 1920, 1934 and 1936 with the concentration of various cemeteries from across the Somme, in 1951 with the addition of the Second World War graves and in 1960-61 with the discovery of several isolated remains. Closed for further burials in 1974.

Lihons:
Creation date: Wartime Cemetery. 1915
6,581 French burials, including 1,638 within four ossuaries.
6 British burials from 1914-18
Extended in 1919, 1935 and 1936 with the concentration of various cemeteries from across the Somme. Closed for further burials in 1988. Contains the remains of the American poet Alan Seeger of the RMLE, who was killed in action at Belloy on 4 July 1916.

Marcelcave *'Les Buttes'*:
Creation date: Wartime Cemetery. 1916
1,610 French burials
Extended in 1932 and 1936 with the concentration of various cemeteries from across the Somme. Closed for further burials in 1980.

Maucourt:
Creation date: 1920
5,272 French burials, including 1,534 buried in six ossuaries
24 French and 6 British burials from 1939-45
Extended in 1920, 1935 and 1936 with the concentration of various

cemeteries from across the Somme and in 1949-53 with the addition of the Second World War graves.

Maurepas:
Creation date: Wartime Cemetery. 1916
3,657 French burials, including 1,588 within two ossuaries.
1 French civilian, 1 Roumanian and 19 Russians from 1914-18
Extended in 1921 and 1936 with the concentration of various cemeteries from the areas of Maurepas, Suzanne and Albert.

Moislains *'Cimetière de la Charente'*:
Creation date: Wartime Cemetery. 1914
465 French dead, including 366 buried within an ossuary.
Extended in 1923 and 1924. Originally established and maintained by the German Army for the French dead of 28 August 1914.

Rancourt:
Creation date: 1921
8,563 French burials, including 3,240 within four ossuaries.
3 French civilian burials from 1914-18 and 1 French burial from 1939-45
Concentration cemetery formed by the concentration of smaller cemeteries around Combles, Cléry and Curlu. Open for burials of individual remains located on the battlefields between 1945 and 1973. Extended in 1980 with the concentration of isolated graves and *carrés militaires* around Flixécourt and Bus-la-Mesière. Closed for burials between 1987 and 1988.

Villers-Carbonnel:
Creation date: 1920
2,285 French burials, including 1,295 within two ossuaries.
18 French burials from 1940
Concentration cemetery formed by the concentration of smaller cemeteries around Barleux and Flaucourt. Extended by the German Army in 1941 with the burials of the French soldiers from 1940.

Appendix Two

Select Gazetteer of French/British Wartime Nomenclatures

Bois sans Nom	Nameless Wood
Tranchée des Framboises	Casement Trench
Tranchée des Calottes	Horn Alley
Bois Fromage	Cheese Wood
Bois du Sommet	Summit Copse
Bois de l'Observation	Observation Wood
Bois des Ouvrages	Earthworks Copse
Bois Croisette	Howitzer Wood
Bois de Berlingots	Berlin Wood
Bois de Berlinval	Clery Copse
Bois Madame	Road Wood
Ferme du Bois Labé	Quarry Farm
Tranchée de Carlsbad	Lightning Trench (west)
Tranchée de Tirpitz	Lightning Trench (east)
Tranchée de Berlin	Blue Avenue
ouvrage de Tripot	The Nebula
Tranchée de Bois St.Vaast	Forestry Trench
Boyeau de la Faim	Guadeloupe Alley (partly)
Bois Hache	Bull's Wood
Bois de la Vache	Cow's Wood
Garenne Carpezat	Caperat Wood
Garenne Boucher	Boucher Wood
Bois Bosquet	Little Warren
Garenne de l'Hospice	Hospice Wood
Fortin/ouvrage de Biaches	Herbecourt Redoubt
Bois Blaise	Biaches Wood
Bois de Biaches	Grand Wood
Bois Keman	Keman Copse
Bois Etoilé	Starry Wood
Bois du Cerisier	Cherrypicker Copse
Bois du Page	Page Copse

French Ranks (*grades*) and their British Army Equivalents

	French	British
Honourary	Maréchal de France	
General Officers	Maréchal Général de groupe d'Armées Général d'Armée* Général de corps d'Armée* Général de division Général de brigade	Field Marshal General Lieutenant General Major General Brigadier General
Officers	Colonel Lieutenant-Colonel Commandant / Chef de bataillon / Chef d'escadron Capitaine Lieutenant sous-Lieutenant	Colonel Lieutenant Colonel Major Captain Lieutenant Second Lieutenant
Officer trainees	Aspirant Élève-officier	Officer candidate Officer cadet
Warrant Officers	Adjudant-chef Adjudant	Warrant Officer Class I Warrant Officer Class II
N.C.O.s	Sergent-chef / Sergent-major / Maréchal des Logis-chef Sergent-fourier** Sergent / Maréchal des Logis	Staff Sergeant ** Sergeant
Other Ranks	Caporal-fourier** Caporal / Brigadier Soldat 1er classe Soldat 2e classe	** Corporal Lance Corporal Private
Role-specific private soldier titles	Chasseur Conducteur Hussard Lancier Marsouin Chacal Dragon Cuirassier Légionnaire Chasseur Cavalier Canonier	
	* As opposed to being a rank, these were titles of *appointement* issued to officers holding the rank of *Général de division*. These appointments indicated seniority over others holding the rank.	** Though there is no real equivalent in the British Army, these ranks would equate to a 'Quartermaster Corporal' and a 'Quartermaster Sergeant'

French Army Abbreviations
1914 – 1918

A.	*Armée*	Army
A.C.	*Artillerie de Corps*	Corps Artillery
A.C.A.	*Artillerie de Corps d'Armée*	Corps Artillery
A.C.D.	*Artillerie de Campagne Divisionnaire*	Divisional Field Artillery
A.C.D.A.	*Artillerie de Corps d'Armée*	Corps Artillery
A.D.	*Artillerie Divisionnaire*	Divisional Artillery
A.L.	*Artillerie Lourde*	Heavy Artillery
A.L.C	*Artillerie Légère de Campagne*	Light Field Artillery
A.L.C.A.	*Artillerie Lourde de Corps d'Armée*	Corps Heavy Artillery
A.L.D.	*Artillerie Lourde Divisionnaire*	Divisional Heavy Artillery
A.L.G.P.	*Artillerie Lourde à Grande Portée*	Long Range Heavy Artillery
A.L.V.F.	*Artillerie Lourde sur Voie Ferrée*	Heavy Railway Artillery
A.M.	*Auto-Mitrailleuse*	Armoured Car
Amb.	*Ambulance*	Ambulance
A.M.C.	*Auto-Mitrailleuse de Cavalerie*	Cavalry Armoured Cars
A.R.S.	*Appareil Respiratoire Spécial*	Respirator (int. 1918)
Art.	*Artillerie*	Artillery
A.S.	*Artillerie Spéciale*	Special Artillery (Tanks)
A.T.	*Artillerie de Tranchées*	Trench Artillery
B.	*Bataillon*	Battalion
Bat.	*Bataillon*	Battalion
B.C.A.	*Bataillon de Chasseurs Alpins*	Mountain Light Infantry Battalion
B.C.P.	*Bataillon de Chasseurs à Pied*	Light Infantry Battalion

Bde.	*Brigade*	Brigade
B.I.	*Bataillon d'Infanterie*	Infantry Battalion
Bie.	*Batterie*	Battery
B.I.L.A	*Bataillon d'Infanterie Légère d'Afrique*	African Light Infantry
B.M.	*Bataillon de Mitrailleurs*	Machine gun battalion
Brig.	*Brigade*	Brigade
B.T.C.A.	*Bataillon Territorial de Chasseurs Alpins*	Territorial Mountain Light Infantry
Btn./Baon.	*Bataillon*	Battalion
Btn.M.	*Bataillon de Mitrailleuses*	Machine gun battalion
B.T.S.	*Bataillon de Tirailleurs Sénégalais*	Senegalese Riflemen Battalion
C.A.	*Corps d'armée*	Army Corps
C.A.C.	*Corps d'armée colonial*	Colonial Army Corps
C.A.I.	*Corps d'armée Italien*	Italian Army Corps
C.A.P.	*Corps d'armée Provisoire*	Provisional Army Corps
Cav.	*Cavalerie*	Cavalry
C.C.	*Corps de cavalerie*	Cavalry Corps
C.E.P.	*Corps Expéditionnaire Portugais*	Portuguese Expeditionary Corps
C.E.O.	*Compagnie d'equipages d'ouvrages*	Fortress Garrison Company
Chass.d'Af.	*Chasseurs d'Afrique*	Army of Africa Light Cavalry
C.H.R.	*Compagnie Hors-Rang*	Regimental Administration Company
C.I.D.	*Centre d'Instruction Divisionnaire*	Divisional Training Centre
Cie.	*Compagnie*	Company
Cie.T.	*Compagnie de Télégraphistes*	Telegraphist company
C.M.	*Compagnie de Mitrailleuses*	Machine gun company
Cuir.	*Cuirassiers*	Cuirassiers (Cavalry)

D.C.	*Division de Cavalerie*	Cavalry Division
D.C.A.	*Défense Contre Avions*	Anti - aircraft defences
D.C.P.	*Division de Cavalerie à Pied*	Foot Cavalry Division
D.D.	*Dépôt Divisionnaire*	Divisional Depot
Dét.	*Détachement*	Detachment
D.I.	*Division d'Infanterie*	Infantry Division
D.I.C.	*Division d'Infanterie Coloniale*	Colonial Infantry Division
D.I.P.	*Division d'Infanterie Provisoire*	Provisional Infantry Division
D.I.R.	*Division d'Infanterie de Réserve*	Reserve Infantry Division
D.I.T.	*Division d'Infanterie Territoriale*	Territorial Infantry Division
D.M.	*Division Marocaine*	Moroccan Division
D.R.	*Division de Réserve*	Reserve Division
Drag.	*Dragons*	Dragoons (Cavalry)
D.T.	*Division Territoriale*	Territorial Division
D.T.	*Détachement de Télégraphistes*	Telegraph Detachment
E.M.	*État-major*	Staff (or Headquarters)
E.R.D.	*Équipe de Réparation de Division*	Divisional Salvage and Repair
Esc.	*Escadron*	Squadron
Esc.	*Escadrille*	Squadron
E.S.M.	*École Spéciale Militaire (Saint-Cyr)*	Military Academy (Saint-Cyr)
F.A.	*Forces Aériennes*	Aerial forces
F.M.	*Fusil Mitrailleur*	Light Machine Gun
F.M.	*Fusilier Marin*	Naval Infantry
G.A.	*Groupe d'Armées*	Army Group
G.A.C.	*Groupe d'Armées du Centre*	Army Group Center
G.A.E.	*Groupe d'Armées de l'Est*	Army Group East
G.A.F.	*Groupe d'Armées des Flandres*	Army Group Flanders
G.A.N.	*Groupe d'Armées du Nord*	Army Group North
G.A.P.	*Groupe des Armées de Paris*	Army Group Paris

G.A.R.	*Groupe d'Armées de Réserve*	Reserve Army Group
G.B.C.	*Groupe de Batteries de Corps*	Corps Artillery Battery Group
G.B.C.	*Groupe de Brancardiers de Corps*	Corps Stretcher-bearer group
G.B.D.	*Groupe de Brancardiers Divisionnaire*	Divisional Stretcher-bearer group
G.D.I.	*Groupe de Divisions d'Infanterie*	Group of Infantry Divisions
G.D.R.	*Groupe de Divisions de Réserve*	Group of Reserve Divisions
G.D.T.	*Groupe de Divisions Territoriales*	Group of Territorial Divisions
G.E.	*Groupe d'Exploitation*	Divisional Operations Group
G.Q.G.	*Grand Quartier Général*	Supreme Head Quarters
G.Q.G.A.	*Grand Quartier Général des Armées Alliées*	Supreme Head Quarters of Allied Armies
Gr.	*Groupe*	Group
I.D.	*Infanterie Divisionnaire*	Divisional Infantry
Inf.	*Infanterie*	Infantry
P.A.	*Parc d'Artillerie*	Artillery Park
P.A.C.A.	*Parc d'Artillerie de Corps d'Armée*	Army Corps Artiilery Park
P.A.D.	*Parc d'Artillerie Divisionnaire*	Divisional Artillery Park
P.C.	*Poste de Commandement*	Command Post
P.O.	*Poste d'Observation*	Observation Post
P.R.	*Point de Résistance*	Strong point
P.S.D.	*Poste de Secours Divisionnaire*	Divisional Aid Post
P.S.R.	*Poste de Secours Régimentaire*	Regimental Aid Post
Q.G.	*Quartier Général*	Head Quarters
R.A.	*Régiment d'Artillerie*	Artillery Regiment
R.A.C.	*Régiment d'Artillerie de Campagne*	Field Artillery Regiment
R.A.C.C.	*Régiment d'Artillerie de Campagne Coloniale*	Colonial Field Artillery Regiment

R.A.D.	*Régiment d'Artillerie Divisionnaire*	Divisional Artillery Regiment
R.A.L.	*Régiment d'Artillerie Lourde*	Heavy Artillery Regiment
R.A.P.	*Régiment d'Artillerie à Pied*	Foot Artillery Regiment
R.C.A.	*Régiment de Chasseurs d'Afrique*	African Light Cavalry Regiment
R.C.C.	*Régiment de Chars de Combat*	Tank regiment
R.D.	*Réserve de Division*	Divisional Reserve
R.E.	*Régiment Étranger*	Foreign Regiment (Foreign Legion)
R.G.A.	*Réserve Générale d'Artillerie*	General Artillery reserve
R.G.A.L.	*Réserve Générale d'Artillerie Lourde*	General Heavy Artillery reserve
Rgt.	*Régiment*	Regiment
R.I.	*Régiment d'Infanterie*	Infantry Regiment
R.I.C.	*Régiment d'Infanterie Coloniale*	Colonial Infantry Regiment
R.I.C.M.	*Régiment d'Infanterie Coloniale du Maroc*	Moroccan Infantry Regiment
R.I.R.	*Régiment d'Infanterie de Réserve*	Reserve Infantry Regiment
R.I.T.	*Régiment d'Infanterie Territoriale*	Territorial Infantry Regiment
R.M.	*Régiment de Marche*	Provisional Regiment
R.M.A.	*Régiment de Marche d'Afrique*	African Provisional Regiment
R.M.L.E.	*Régiment de Marche de la Légion Étrangère*	Foreign Legion Provisional Regiment
R.M.T.	*Régiment de Marche de Tirailleurs*	Provisional Regiment of Tirailleurs
R.M.T.A.	*Régiment de Marche de Tirailleurs Algériens*	Provisional Regiment of Algerian Tirailleurs
R.M.T.I.	*Régiment de Marche de Tirailleurs Indigènes*	Provisional Regiment Indigenous Tirailleurs

226

R.M.Z.	*Régiment de Marche de Zouaves*	Provisional Regiment of Zouaves
R.M.Z.T.	*Régiment Mixte de Zouaves et Tirailleurs*	Combined Zouave-Tirailleur Regiment
R.S.A.	*Régiment de Spahis Algériens*	Regiment of Algerian Cavalry
R.S.M.	*Régiment de Spahis Marocains*	Regiment of Moroccan Cavalry
R.T.A.	*Régiment de Tirailleurs Algériens*	Regiment of Algerian Riflemen
R.T.I.	*Régiment de Tirailleurs Indigènes*	Regiment of Indigenous Riflemen
R.T.M.	*Régiment de Tirailleurs Marocains*	Regiment of Moroccan Riflemen
R.T.N.A.	*Régiment de Tirailleurs Nord-Africains*	Regiment of North African Riflemen
R.T.S.	*Régiment de Tirailleurs Sénégalais*	Regiment of Senegalese Riflemen
R.T.T.	*Régiment de Tirailleurs Tunisiens*	Regiment of Tunisian Riflemen
S.C.O.A.	*Section de Commis et Ouvriers d'Administration*	Section of clerks and administration
Sect.	*Secteur (ou Section)*	Sector or Section
S.O.A.	*Section d'Ouvriers d'Administration*	Administration Section
S.O.A.	*Section d'Ouvriers d'Artillerie*	Artillery labourer section
S.M.A.	*Section de Munitions d'Artillerie*	Artillery Ammunition Supply Section
S.M.I.	*Section de Munitions d'Infanterie*	Infantry Ammunition Supply Platoon
S.M.I.	*Section de Mitrailleuses d'Infanterie*	Infantry machine gun platoon
S.O.	*Sous-Officier*	Non-commissioned Officer
S.P.	*Section de Projecteurs*	Trench Mortar Platoon
S.R.	*Service de Renseignements*	Intelligence Service

S.R.A.	*Section de Ravitaillement d'Artillerie*	Artillery Supply Section
S.S.	*Service de Santé*	Medical Service
S.S.A,	*Section Sanitaire Automobile*	Motor-ambulance section
S.S.A.A.	*Section Sanitaire Automobile Anglaise*	English (volunteer) motor-ambulance
S.S.U.	*Section Sanitaire automobile américaine*	American (volunteer) motor-ambulance
S.T.A.	*Section de Transport Automobile*	Motor transport section
S.T.D.I.	*Section Topographique de Division d'Infanterie*	Divisional Topographical section
T.R	*Train Régimentaire*	Regimental Supply Train
T.S.F	*Télégraphie Sans Fil*	Wireless telegraphy
V.B	*Vivien Bessière*	Rifle Grenade
V.F.	*Voie Ferrée*	Rail Track

Appendix Five:

French Orders of Battle
1914 – 1918

1ˢᵗ July 1916 Divisional Order of Assault – north to south
39ᵉ Division d'infanterie
11ᵉ Division d'infanterie

RIVER SOMME AND SOMME CANAL
16ᵉ Division d'infanterie coloniale (one regiment)
2ᵉ Division d'infanterie coloniale
3ᵉ Division d'infanterie coloniale
61ᵉ Division d'infanterie.
51ᵉ Division d'infanterie (partial…. Not involved in the attack)

Divisions holding the line to the immediate south of the 1st July 'zone'
as far as Marquevillers...

51ᵉ Division d'infanterie (partial)
58ᵉ Division d'infanterie
62ᵉ Division d'infanterie
10e Division d'infanterie coloniale

1ˢᵗ July 1916 Regimental Order of Assault - north to south:
17th Bn King's (Liverpool) Regiment (30th Division, British)
153ᵉ Régiment d'infanterie
146ᵉ Régiment d'infanterie
156ᵉ Régiment d'infanterie
26ᵉ Régiment d'infanterie
69ᵉ Régiment d'infanterie
79ᵉ Régiment d'infanterie
37ᵉ Régiment d'infanterie

RIVER SOMME AND SOMME CANAL
36ᵉ Régiment d'infanterie coloniale
22ᵉ Régiment d'infanterie coloniale
24ᵉ Régiment d'infanterie coloniale

4ᵉ Régiment d'infanterie coloniale
8ᵉ Régiment d'infanterie coloniale
23ᵉ Régiment d'infanterie coloniale
21ᵉ Régiment d'infanterie coloniale
58ᵉ Régiment d'infanterie coloniale
7ᵉ Régiment d'infanterie coloniale
265ᵉ Régiment d'infanterie
264ᵉ Régiment d'infanterie
219ᵉ Régiment d'infanterie
262ᵉ Régiment d'infanterie

French Corps on the Somme, July to December 1916

1ᵉ Corps d'armée	(Guillaumat)
2ᵉ Corps d'armée	(Duchêne)
5ᵉ Corps d'armée	(Baucheron de Boissoudy)
6ᵉ Corps d'armée	(Paulinier)
7e Corps d'armée	(de Bazelaire)
9ᵉ Corps d'armée	(Pentel)
11ᵉ Corps d'armée	(Mangin)
20ᵉ Corps d'armée	(Claret de la Touche and Mazillier)
21ᵉ Corps d'armée	(Maistre)
30ᵉ Corps d'armée	(Chrétien)
32ᵉ Corps d'armée	(Berthelot and Debeney)
33ᵉ Corps d'armée	(Nudant)
35ᵉ Corps d'armée	(Jacquot)
1ᵉ Corps d'armée coloniale	(Berdoulat)
2ᵉ Corps d'armée coloniale	(Blondlat)
1ᵉ Corps de cavalerie	(Conneau)
2ᵉ Corps de cavalerie	(de Mitry)

French Divisions on the Somme, July to December 1916

1e Division d'infanterie
2e Division d'infanterie
3e Division d'infanterie
4e Division d'infanterie
10e Division d'infanterie
11e Division d'infanterie
12e Division d'infanterie
13e Division d'infanterie
14e Division d'infanterie
17e Division d'infanterie
18e Division d'infanterie

20e Division d'infanterie
25e Division d'infanterie
26e Division d'infanterie
39e Division d'infanterie
41e Division d'infanterie
42e Division d'infanterie
43e Division d'infanterie
45e Division d'infanterie
46e Division d'infanterie
47e Division d'infanterie
48e Division d'infanterie
51e Division d'infanterie
53e Division d'infanterie
56e Division d'infanterie
61e Division d'infanterie
62e Division d'infanterie
66e Division d'infanterie
70e Division d'infanterie
72e Division d'infanterie
77e Division d'infanterie
120e Division d'infanterie
121e Division d'infanterie
125e Division d'infanterie
127e Division d'infanterie
132e Division d'infanterie
152e Division d'infanterie
153e Division d'infanterie
Division Morocaine
2e Division d'infanterie coloniale
3e Division d'infanterie coloniale
10e Division d'infanterie coloniale
15e Division d'infanterie coloniale
16e Division d'infanterie coloniale

Cavalry Divisions
1e Division de cavalerie
2e Division de cavalerie
3e Division de cavalerie
4e Division de cavalerie

Select Sources and Bibliography

French Language Sources

14-18 Magazine No.73 '1916 – la Somme': Hommell Magazines, May/June/July 2016

Atlas des Nécropoles Nationales : Ministère des anciens combattants et victimes de guerre, La documentation Français, 1994

De la Mort à la Mémoire : Yann, Thomas, OREP Editions, 2008

Guide des Cimetiéres Militaires en France : Grive –Santini, Catherine, le cherche midi éditeur, 1999

Guide Michelin Les champs de bataille 1914 – 1918 - Somme (Amiens, Péronne, Albert) : Michelin & Cie./ECPAD, 2014

Journal Militaire officiel: Librairie Militaire R.Chapelot et Cie., Paris (various years 1899 – 1914)

La bataille de la Somme juillet – novembre 1916 : Denizot, Alain. Tempus, 2006

La Somme – l'offensive tragique : Thers, Alexandre, Histoire & Collections, 2002

Les Armées Françaises dans la Grande Guerre, Tome IV 'Verdun et la Somme', Vols. 2 & 3 : Service Historique, Ministére de la Guerre, 1926

Les Armées Françaises dans la Grande Guerre, Tome X , Ordres de bataille des grandes unités Vol.1 : Service Historique, Ministére de la Guerre, 1923

Les Armées Françaises dans la Grande Guerre, Tome X , Ordres de bataille des grandes unités Vol.2 - Divisions d'infanterie & Divisions d'cavalerie : Service Historique, Ministére de la Guerre, 1924

La Grande Guerre sur le Front Occidental, Vol XI – Bataille de la Somme : Palat, général Barthelemy-Edmond, Berger-Levrault, 1925

Mort au Combat! :Vauclair, Gilles, Editions-Sutton, 2015

Tranchées Magazine Hors série No.3 'Juillet 1916 – Verdun & la Somme' : Ysec Éditions, July 2012

Tranchées Magazine No.26 'Centenaire 1916 – Verdun & la Somme' : Ysec Éditions, July/August/September 2016

Regimental Histories :

42ᵉ Régiment d'infanterie –Historique Sommaire pendant la Grande Guerre : (regimentally published, undated)

63ᵉ Régiment d'infanterie –Historique Sommaire du Régiment : (regimentally published, undated)

'Arraõk – en Avant!' - Historique du 262ᵉ Régiment d'infanterie : Charles Lavauzelle et cie, Paris 1921

Historique Abrégé du 3ᵉ Battailon du chasseurs â pied pendant la Guerre 1914-1918 : Berger-Levrault, Nancy-Paris-Strasbourg (undated)

Historique du 2ᵉ Régiment d'infanterie : Henri Charles-Lavauzelle, Paris, 1920

Historique du 4ᵉ Régiment d'infanterie coloniale : B. Bouchet, Toulon (undated)

Historique du 5ᵉ Régiment d'infanterie : Henri Charles-Lavauzelle, Paris, 1920

Historique du 21ᵉ Colonial 1914-18 : A. Davy et fils Aîné, Paris, 1920

Historique du 22ᵉ Régiment d'infanterie coloniale pendant la Guerre 1914-1918 : Berger-Levrault, Nancy-Paris-Strasbourg (undated)

Historique du 23ᵉ Régiment d'infanterie coloniale pendant la Guerre 1914-1918 : Berger-Levrault, Nancy-Paris-Strasbourg (undated)

Historique du 24ᵉ Régiment d'infanterie coloniale : Barriére et cie, Perpignan, 1920

Historique du 25ᵉ Régiment d'infanterie : Librairie Chapelot, Paris (undated)

Historique du 26ᵉ Régiment d'infanterie pendant la Guerre 1914-1918 : Berger-Levrault, Nancy-Paris-Strasbourg (undated)

Historique du 36ᵉ Régiment d'infanterie coloniale pendant la Guerre 1914-1918 : Berger-Levrault, Nancy-Paris-Strasbourg (1920)

Historique du 37ᵉ Régiment d'infanterie coloniale pendant la Guerre 1914-1918 : Berger-Levrault, Nancy-Paris-Strasbourg (undated)

Historique du 43ᵉ Bataillon de chasseurs â pied pendant la Guerre 1914-1918 : Berger-Levrault, Nancy-Paris-Strasbourg (undated)

Historique du 58ᵉ Régiment d'infanterie coloniale pendant la Grande Guerre 1914-1918 : Mouton & Combe, Toulon, 1921

Historique du 69ᵉ Régiment d'infanterie : Librairie Chapelot, Paris (undated)

Historique du 75ᵉ Régiment d'infanterie - Campagne 1914-18 : Berger-Levrault, Nancy-Paris-Strasbourg (undated)

Historique du 91ᵉ Régiment d'infanterie pendant la Campagne 1914-18 : A. Ancieux, Charleville, 1920

Historique du 146ᵉ Régiment d'infanterie: Berger-Levrault, Nancy-Paris-Strasbourg (undated)

Historique du 160ᵉ Régiment d'infanterie, Campagne 1914-18 : Réunies de Nancy, 1920

Historique du 164ᵉ Régiment d'infanterie - Campagne 1914-18 : Chapelot, Paris (undated)

Historique du 170ᵉ Régiment d'infanterie : Faivre d'Arcier, 1919
Historique du 264ᵉ Régiment d'infanterie : P. Demange, Angers, 1920
Historique du Régiment de Marche de la Légion Étrangère : Berger-
   Levrault, Paris (undated)
*Le 7ᵉ Bataillon de chasseurs alpins pendant la Grande Guerre 1914-
   1918 :* Olivier Joulian, Draguignan, 1920
Le 7ᵉ Régiment d'infanterie coloniale dans la Grande Guerre : G
   Delmas, Bordeaux (undated)
Le 17ᵉ Régiment d'infanterie, le Régiment d'Auvergne de 1914 à 1918 :
   Wayer et Josse, Prémery, Nièvre (undated)
*Le Régiment Rose – Histoire du 265ᵉ Régiment d'infanterie, 1914-
   1919* : du Plessis, Jean. Payot, Paris, 1920.
Les Grandes Journées du 153ᵉ Régiment d'infanterie : Paul Kahn,
   Épinal, 1920
Le Quinze-six pendant la Grande Guerre : Berger-Levrault, Nancy-
   Paris-Strasbourg (undated)
Un régiment de Lorraine – Le 79ᵉ , Verdun-la Somme : Mangin, E.
   Payot, Paris, 1934.

***Journaux des marches et opérations (J.M.O.s)* – French War Diaries**
The vast majority of these are on the *Mémoire des hommes* website
owned and maintained by the *Service historique de la Défense* (a section
of the *Ministère de la Défense*). They can be freely accessed at the
following website: http://www.memoiredeshommes.sga.defense. gouv.fr

English Language Sources
Before Endeavours Fade: Coombs, Rose E.B., After the Battle, (12ᵗʰ
   edition) 2006
Bloody Victory – The Sacrifice on the Somme: Philpott, William.
   Abacus, 2010
Handbook of the French Army 1914: General Staff, War Office, 1914
   (reprinted by IWM & Battery Press, 1995)
Letters and Diary of Alan Seeger: Seeger, Alan. Charles Scribner &
   Sons, 1917
Major & Mrs. Holt's Definitive Battlefield Guide to the Somme: Holt,
   Tonie & Valmai, Pen & Sword, 2016
*History of the Great War Based on Official Documents - Military
   Operations: France and Belgium 1916 Vol.1 :* Edmonds, Brig.Gen.
   Sir James E, Macmillan & Co. Ltd , 1932
*History of the Great War Based on Official Documents - Military
   Operations: France and Belgium 1916 Vol.2* : Miles, Capt.Wilfred,
   Macmillan & Co. Ltd, 1938

Paths of Glory – The French Army 1914-18: Clayton, Anthony. Cassell, 2003

Pyrrhic Victory: Doughty, Robert A. Harvard University Press, 2008

Somme 1916 – a Battlefield Companion: Gliddon, Gerald. The History Press, 2009

Somme – 1ˢᵗ July 1916, Tragedy and Triumph : Robertshaw, Andrew. Osprey (Campaign), 2006

The Battle of the Somme: Strohn, Matthias (ed.), Osprey, 2016

The French Army 1914-18: Sumner, Ian, Osprey (Men at Arms), 1995

The French Army and the First World War: Greenhalgh, Elizabeth, Cambridge University Press, 2014

The German Army on the Somme 1914 -1916: Sheldon, Jack, Pen and Sword, 2007

The Illustrated Michelin Guides to the Battlefields – The Somme Vol.1: Michelin & Cie., 1919

The March to the Marne – The French Army 1871-1914: Porch, Douglas, Cambridge Univesity Press, 1981

The Middlebrook Guide to the Somme Battlefields: Middlebrook, Martin & Mary, Viking 1991

German Language Sources

Am Rande der Strassen – Frankreich, Belgien, Luxemburg und Niederlande : Volksbund Deutsche Kriegsgräberfürsorge e.V., 1989

Der Weltkrieg 1914 bis 1918 : Band 10 - Die Operationen des Jahres 1916 : bis zum Wechsel in der Obersten Heeresleitung : Mittler, Berlin 1936

Der Weltkrieg 1914 bis 1918 : Band 11 - Die Kriegsführung im Herbst 1916 und im Winter 1916/17 : vom Wechsel in der Obersten Heeresleitung bis zum Entschluß zum Rückzug in die Siegfried-Stellung : Mittler, Berlin 1936

Militärgeschichtlicher Reiseführer zu den Schlachtfeldern des Ersten Weltkrieges in Flandern und Nordfrankreich : Klauer, Markus, 2004

Schlachten des Weltkrieges Band 20, Somme-Nord, I Teil : von Stosch, Albrecht (ed.), Gerhard Stalling, 1927

Schlachten des Weltkrieges Band 21, Somme-Nord, II Teil : von Stosch, Albrecht (ed.), Gerhard Stalling, 1927

Index